普通高等学校"十四五"规划英语语言文学类专业新形态教材

Advanced English Reading

高级英语阅读教程

主　编 ◎ 贾文娟　杜　玮　胡又铭
副主编 ◎ 朱海燕
参编者 ◎ 张燕萍　杨文姣

华中科技大学出版社
http://press.hust.edu.cn
中国·武汉

内 容 提 要

本教材由八个单元构成，借鉴相关领域的教学经验和先进理念，从经济、社会、环境、科技等方面综合讨论了当代中国所取得的各项成就。选取高质量的阅读材料，对提高学生用英语讲述中国故事、中国文化的能力进行针对性的辅导。每个主题都是中国道路、中国理论、中国制度、中国精神和中国力量的生动体现。每个单元有三个阅读语篇，每篇文章后设置了与相应单元思辨阅读技巧密切相关的阅读练习，以帮助学生更充分地理解信息、辨析信息、表达见解和观点。每个单元末都有一项实践任务，旨在增进学生对中国社会的认识和理解，从而使其在讲述中国故事时具有更深入、更生动的材料和体验，让故事更有说服力和吸引力。

图书在版编目(CIP)数据

高级英语阅读教程 / 贾文娟，杜玮，胡又铭主编. -- 武汉：华中科技大学出版社，2024.11. --（普通高等学校"十四五"规划英语语言文学类专业新形态教材）. -- ISBN 978-7-5772-1264-7

Ⅰ．H319.37

中国国家版本馆 CIP 数据核字第 20249JG367 号

高级英语阅读教程　　　　　　　　　　　　　　　　贾文娟　杜　玮　胡又铭　主编
Gaoji Yingyu Yuedu Jiaocheng

策划编辑：宋　焱
责任编辑：刘　凯
封面设计：廖亚萍
责任校对：张汇娟
责任监印：周治超

出版发行：华中科技大学出版社（中国·武汉）　　　电话：(027) 81321913
　　　　　武汉市东湖新技术开发区华工科技园　　　邮编：430223

录　　排：华中科技大学出版社美编室
印　　刷：武汉开心印印刷有限公司
开　　本：787mm×1092mm　1/16
印　　张：13
字　　数：340 千字
版　　次：2024 年 11 月第 1 版第 1 次印刷
定　　价：59.00 元

本书若有印装质量问题，请向出版社营销中心调换
全国免费服务热线：400-6679-118　　竭诚为您服务
版权所有　侵权必究

前言
PREFACE

  习近平在2024年新年贺词中指出："中国不仅发展自己，也积极拥抱世界，担当大国责任。"进入新时代，中国对外开放开启新征程，中国积极拥抱世界，成为世界和平的建设者、全球发展的贡献者、国际秩序的坚定维护者。中国道路、中国的发展引起国际社会前所未有的广泛关注。在这些关注中，存在不同的声音和观点。有些人或组织对中国的发展和成就表示赞赏和支持，认为中国在经济、科技等诸多领域取得巨大进步，中国的崛起，特别是中国的现代化建设具有世界性意义；也有一些人或组织夸大中国发展过程中存在的某些问题，质疑和批评中国。而有效反击针对中国的不实言论，理性对待国际社会对中国的评价；介绍新时代的中国，让国际社会理解中国的发展理念、发展道路、发展成就，更好地展示真实、立体、全面的中国，已经成为新时代赋予外语专业学生的重要使命。本教材的编写初衷就是帮助英语专业学生更好地了解当代中国的发展成就和社会风貌，引导学生通过思辨阅读技巧，培养批判性思维，学会分析、评估不同文化背景下的信息，形成独立的思考和判断，并在此基础上积极提问、讨论，不断锻炼和提升自己用英语理性、清晰、流畅地讲述中国故事、传播中国声音、塑造中国形象的能力。

教材结构

  本教材由八个单元构成，主题分别聚焦政治、经济、外交、社会、环境、法律、科技和全球治理，每个主题都是中国道路、中国理论、中国制度、中国精神和中国力量的生动体现。每个单元有三个阅读语篇，每个语篇后设置了与相应的单元思辨阅读技巧密切相关的阅读练习，以帮助学生更充分地理解信息、辨析信息、表达见解和观点。每个单元末都有一项实践任务，旨在增进学生对中国社会的认识和理解，从而使其在讲述中国故事时具有更深入、更生动的材料和体验，让故事更有说服力和吸引力。每个单元的具体架构如下。

* **二十大报告选摘**：党的二十大报告内容丰富、意义深刻，是指引我们全面建设社会主义现代化国家、全面推进中华民族伟大复兴的行动指南。教材选摘报告中与各单元主题关系紧密的相关论述，以双语形式呈现，通过金句、重点和要点，帮助学生掌握重要话语的英语表达、领会二十大精神，引导青年学生树牢对中国特色社会主义的信念、对中华民族伟大复兴中国梦的信心，从而将个人奋斗融入中华民族伟大复兴的时代洪流。

* **思辨阅读技巧**：思辨能力是学生全面发展的基础。培养大学生的思辨能力是高等教育的核心目标之一。为帮助学生循序渐进地提高思辨阅读能力，教材将思辨阅读分解为八大技巧——active reading, analytical reading, evaluation, interpretation, contextualization, synthesizing, inference, reflection。每个单元在阅读篇章前都设置了技巧讲解，并在阅读篇章后设计了问答、演讲、辩论、讨论等多种题型，引导学生学习思辨技巧，训练、提升思辨能力。

* **读前问题与阅读篇章**：每个单元都编写了读前问题，以引导学生回顾和激活与单元主题相关的背景知识，建立与单元内容相关的联系，为篇章阅读和主动思考做好准备。阅读文章的选取：每个单元前两篇来自我国主流媒体、政府重要文件、国家领导人讲话、专家学者的著作等；第三篇则出自外国学者或机构，旨在为学生提供其他文化背景下的不同视角、观点和表达，从而拓宽学生视野，增强其跨文化理解和交流能力。

* **词汇表与习题**：阅读篇章后附有词汇表，其中既有对生词的中文解释，也有对重要机构名称、人名和篇章涉及的行业术语的解释和说明，目的是便于快速查阅和理解，从而提高阅读速度和阅读流畅度，增强阅读理解能力。阅读篇章后的习题都围绕文章主题和所在单元的思辨阅读技巧展开，任务由简入难，一步步引导学生分析思考，从培养思辨意识逐渐过渡到掌握思辨方法。

* **单元实践任务**：教材设计了采访、调研、演说、政策宣讲、写作投稿、模拟联合国（简称模联）等实践活动，促使学生在亲身实践的过程中认识中国国情、了解中国社会、理性看待中国发展过程中面临的问题与困难，增强学生的沟通能力、应变能力，同时激发学生结合自身专业学习助力国家现代化强国建设的责任感和使命感。

* **拓展资源**：每个单元末都提供了相关著作、皮书、纪录片、访谈节目、学术论文等中英文拓展学习资源，以满足不同学生的信息获取和内容学习需求，帮助学生多角度、更全面地理解中国的发展变化及相关背景知识，启发学生探究故事背

后的文化和根源，促进学生的深入思考和学习体验，激发学生传播中国声音的积极性。

  本教材获宁夏大学教材出版基金资助（030700002408）和宁夏大学外国语学院外国语言文学（重点培育）项目的资金支持，特此致谢！

编 者
2024 年 6 月 30 日

I cannot teach anybody anything,
I can only make them think.
—Socrates

目录
CONTENTS

Unit 1　Politics ·· (001)
　Critical Reading Skill—Active Reading ································· (005)
　Text A　Strong Leadership: The Story of the Communist Party of China ········ (008)
　Text B　How Does China's Whole-Process People's Democracy Work? ······ (014)
　Text C　How to Precisely Convey China's Political Discourse to the West? ··· (019)

Unit 2　Economy ··· (027)
　Critical Reading Skill—Analytical Reading ···························· (030)
　Text A　The Reason Why China's Economy Created a Miracle in Nearly
　　　　　40 Years of Reform and Opening Up ···························· (033)
　Text B　China's Miraculous Achievements in Numbers ················ (039)
　Text C　Seven Segments Shaping China's Consumption Landscape ············· (044)

Unit 3　Diplomacy ·· (053)
　Critical Reading Skill—Evaluation ··· (056)
　Text A　Outlook on China's Foreign Policy on Its Neighborhood in the
　　　　　New Era (Excerpt) ·· (059)
　Text B　Major-Country Diplomacy Benefits the World-At-Large ············ (067)
　Text C　China and Ireland Economic and Finance Cooperation(Excerpt) ········ (071)

Unit 4　Society ··· (079)
　Critical Reading Skill—Interpretation ···································· (083)

	Text A	Poverty Alleviation: China's Experience and Contribution (Excerpt)	(086)
	Text B	MOE Press Conference Presents China's Educational Achievements in 2023 (Excerpt)	(092)
	Text C	8 Reasons Why China is the Most Exciting Healthcare Story in the World Right Now	(098)

Unit 5　Environment ····· (105)

Critical Reading Skill—Contextualization ····· (109)

Text A　World Day to Combat Desertification and Drought: China's Journey of Pushing Green forward, Desertification back ····· (112)

Text B　China's Green Development in the New Era (Excerpt) ····· (116)

Text C　Earth Day a Reminder of Our Shared Obligation ····· (121)

Unit 6　Law ····· (127)

Critical Reading Skill—Synthesizing ····· (131)

Text A　China's Law-Based Cyberspace Governance in the New Era (Excerpt) ····· (134)

Text B　Judicial Reform Promotes Rule of Law ····· (138)

Text C　International Law for the Global Community of Shared Future ····· (141)

Unit 7　Science and Technology ····· (147)

Critical Reading Skill—Inference ····· (150)

Text A　Global AI Governance Initiative ····· (153)

Text B　China's Space Program: A 2021 Perspective (Excerpt) ····· (158)

Text C　Xiaomi (Excerpt) ····· (165)

Unit 8　China and Global Governance ····· (171)

Critical Reading Skill—Reflection ····· (175)

Text A　China's Unique Role in the Field of Global Health (Excerpt) ····· (178)

Text B　China's International Development Cooperation in the New Era (Excerpt) ····· (184)

Text C　Understanding China's Growing Involvement in Global Health and Managing Processes of Change (Excerpt) ····· (191)

Unit 1

Politics

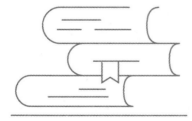

二十大报告选摘

Report to the 20th National Congress of the Communist Party of China (Excerpt)

中国共产党已走过百年奋斗历程。我们党立志于中华民族千秋伟业,致力于人类和平与发展崇高事业,责任无比重大,使命无上光荣。全党同志务必不忘初心、牢记使命,务必谦虚谨慎、艰苦奋斗,务必敢于斗争、善于斗争,坚定历史自信,增强历史主动,谱写新时代中国特色社会主义更加绚丽的华章。

Since its founding a century ago, the Communist Party of China has taken a remarkable journey. Our Party has dedicated itself to achieving lasting greatness for the Chinese nation and committed itself to the noble cause of peace and development for humanity. Our responsibility is unmatched in importance, and our mission is glorious beyond compare. It is imperative that all of us in the Party never forget our original aspiration and founding mission, that we always stay modest, prudent, and hard-working, and that we have the courage and ability to carry on our fight. We must remain confident in our history, exhibit greater historical initiative, and write an even more magnificent chapter for socialism with Chinese characteristics in the new era.

我们全面加强党的领导,明确中国特色社会主义最本质的特征是中国共产党领导,中国特色社会主义制度的最大优势是中国共产党领导,中国共产党是最高政治领导力量,坚持党中央集中统一领导是最高政治原则,系统完善党的领导制度体系,全党增强"四个意识",自觉在思想上政治上行动上同党中央保持高度一致,不断提高政治判断力、政治领悟力、政治执行力,确保党中央权威和集中统一领导,确保党发挥总揽全局、协调各方的领导核心作用,我们这个拥有九千六百多万名党员的马克思主义政党更加团结统一。

We have strengthened Party leadership in all respects. We have made clear that the leadership of the Communist Party of China is the defining feature of socialism with Chinese characteristics and the greatest strength of the system of socialism with Chinese characteristics, that the Party is the highest force of political leadership, and that upholding the centralized, unified leadership of the Party Central Committee is the highest political principle. We have made systematic improvements to the Party's leadership systems. All Party members have become more conscious of the need to maintain political integrity, think in big-picture terms, follow the leadership core, and keep in alignment with the central Party leadership. They have become more purposeful in closely following the Party Central Committee in thinking, political stance, and action, and they have continued to improve their capacity for political judgment, thinking, and implementation. All this has ensured the Party Central Committee's authority and its centralized, unified leadership and guaranteed that the Party fulfills its core role of exercising overall leadership and coordinating the efforts of all sides. Now, our Marxist party of over 96 million members enjoys greater unity and solidarity than ever.

坚持和加强党的全面领导。坚决维护党中央权威和集中统一领导,把党的领导落实到党和国家事业各领域各方面各环节,使党始终成为风雨来袭时全体人民最可靠的主心骨,确保我国社会主义现代化建设正确方向,确保拥有团结奋斗的强大政治凝聚力、发展自信心,集聚起万众一心、共克时艰的磅礴力量。

Upholding and strengthening the Party's overall leadership. We must resolutely uphold the Party Central Committee's authority and its centralized, unified leadership and see that Party leadership is exercised in all aspects and every stage of the endeavors of the Party and the country. This will ensure that our Party always remains the pillar that the Chinese people can lean on in times of difficulty, that our socialist modernization advances along the right path, and that we have the political cohesion and confidence in our development to inspire the people to strive in unity. It will see us forming a mighty force to overcome all difficulties with one heart and one mind.

Critical Reading Skill—Active Reading

Why is active reading important for critical reading?

Active reading involves engaging with the text in a dynamic and focused manner. It is important for critical reading because it helps us to fully understand and analyze the text. By actively engaging with the material, we are able to identify key ideas, evaluate arguments, and draw connections between different parts of the text. This level of engagement allows us to think critically about the author's message, consider alternative perspectives, and form our own opinions. Active reading also helps us to retain information more effectively. By actively processing the material through techniques such as summarizing and note-taking, we are more likely to remember key points and concepts. This not only enhances comprehension but also enables us to engage in deeper analysis and interpretation of the text. Active reading encourages mindful and focused reading. By actively participating in the reading process, we are less likely to passively consume information and more likely to actively think about and engage with the material. This level of engagement is essential for developing critical thinking skills and fostering a deeper understanding of complex ideas.

Tips to train and develop active reading skill:

Active reading is relevant beyond the classroom. Professionals in fields such as law, research, journalism, and academia rely on active reading to comprehend complex documents, analyze arguments, and extract vital information. Students with strong active reading skills can lead to better comprehension, improved critical thinking, and higher performance. Skills cultivated through active reading—such as analysis, interpretation, and effective communication—are transferable to various aspects of our academic and professional lives. This can include applications in writing, public speaking, and critical analysis of media and information. Thus, what should we do to develop active reading?

(1) Set specific goals. Whether it's to understand the author's intention, opinion,

identify the theme, or analyze the author's writing style, having a clear purpose in mind can focus your reading efforts.

(2) Annotate texts. While reading an article or a book, actively annotate the text by highlighting key points, underlining important words, and jotting down notes in the margins. This helps you to identify key ideas, track our thoughts, and make connections within the text.

(3) Engage in pre-reading activities. Preview the text before diving into a full reading. This may involve scanning headings, subheadings, and introductory and concluding paragraphs to gain an overview of the content and structure.

(4) Summarize and paraphrase. Condense what you read into your own words. This process helps reinforce understanding and promotes active engagement with the material.

(5) Reflect and discuss. Connect the text with your own experiences, other texts, or current events. Critically analyze the author's arguments, tone, and potential biases. Evaluate the text's strengths, weaknesses, and underlying assumptions. Then articulate your thinking, interpretations and questions about the text. Having dialogues and discussion with others can further enhance your understanding.

Warm-up Questions

1. What are some of the keywords you can use to describe the Communist Party of China?
2. What is behind the success of the Communist Party of China?
3. Do you know how is China's whole-process people's democracy practiced?

Text

Strong Leadership: The Story of the Communist Party of China

Founded in 1921, the Communist Party of China (CPC), from day one, has always been committed to its original aspiration and mission of seeking happiness for the Chinese people and rejuvenation for the Chinese nation. Over the past 100 years, the CPC has resolutely led the people through arduous and bitter fights, leaving behind a fascinating collection of epic stories. In 2020, China reached almost 101.6 trillion RMB in GDP, with the per capita exceeding 10,000 USD. Its economy, technology, and overall national strength have advanced to a new level. With its people living a considerably happier life, China brings about the historic achievement of building a moderately prosperous society. A country cannot prosper without a capable political party, and a political party cannot grow without strong leaders. China's success is essentially attributable to the CPC's solid leadership that guides the course.

Since the inception of the CPC, Chinese communists with Comrade Mao Zedong as the shining epitome have combined the basic tenets of Marxism-Leninism with the particular case of China's revolution. They have successfully encircled cities by the countryside and seized political power through military force. From their victory over Japanese imperialism and Kuomintang's reactionary rule emerged the People's Republic of China. Since the People's Republic of China was founded, they continued to lead the Chinese people through the Socialist Revolution, which facilitated an independent and sound industrial system and national economy to take shape. It has laid the political and institutional foundation for China's contemporary development and provided valuable lessons as well as ideological and material basis for the proposal of socialism with Chinese characteristics. After 1978, Chinese communists with Comrade Deng Xiaoping as the chief representative liberated their minds and sought truth from facts. They made the historic decision to shift the focus of the CPC and the state to economic development and kicked off the reform and opening up program. They established Deng Xiaoping Theory, calling for a China-specific development path and socialism with Chinese characteristics, which proved to be a great success. Then, the Theory of Three Represents and the Scientific Outlook on Development emerged one after another, which upheld and developed socialism with Chinese characteristics under new circumstances.

Since 2012, Chinese communists with Comrade Xi Jinping as the core of the leadership have been well aware of the need to reposition their socialist theories in line with the changes of the times and the concurrent priorities and initiatives. They established Xi Jinping Thought on Socialism with Chinese Characteristics for a New Era to promote balanced political, economic, cultural, social and ecological development. "Four Comprehensives", specifically, building a moderately prosperous society in all respects, deepening reforms across-the-board, advancing law-based governance in a well-rounded manner and tightening party discipline at every nook and cranny, have become on top of the country's strategic agenda. They have also striven for the modernization of China's governance system and capabilities and worked diligently to make people feel satisfied, happier and secure. They have found solutions to many long-overdue challenges and cleared the backlog of major initiatives. These historic changes and accomplishments bring bright prospects for the renewal of the Chinese nation. In retrospect, General Secretary Xi has shown unwavering convictions, people-centered values and strong will as the Party's core, people's leader and military commander. He is the embodiment of selfless dedication to the good of the people. In return, he has won the universal support from members of the Party, the people and the military, complemented by international recognition.

The CPC's centennial history is featured by the theme of tireless struggle, ideological exploration and internal development. Over its century-old life, CPC has constantly committed itself to the happiness of Chinese people, the rejuvenation of the Chinese nation and the common good of the world.

First, the CPC is committed to exploring the development path aligned with China's realities. "What is a road? It is something trampled out of a place where once there was no road; it is made from a place where once there were only brambles and thickets," said Lu Xun, a celebrated Chinese writer. The Party adapts the basic principles of Marxism to China's conditions to make it more compatible with the country's modern context. Xi Jinping Thought on Socialism with Chinese Characteristics for a New Era is the Marxism for contemporary China in the 21st century with significant influence both at home and abroad. It diversifies the options for the modernization of the developing world by presenting an alternative for the countries and nations that aspire for faster growth without compromising independence, providing inputs to this mankind's challenge with a Chinese solution. Omari, former Secretary General of Morocco's Authenticity and Modernity Party, said that a country cannot indiscriminately copy the practice of other countries, but China's development path brings a new line of hope for the developing countries with a thirst for modernization.

Second, the CPC upholds the fundamental stance of siding with the people. With delivering a better life to the people as its ultimate mission, the CPC gives full scope to the people to create historical achievements. General Secretary Xi stressed that, "the history has made it crystal clear that a government's top priority should be its people; people are the very foundation of a government; people's support is a matter of life and death for the Party." Since 2012, General Secretary Xi Jinping has personally led the battle against poverty, promoting targeted and effective actions with unprecedented commitment and resolve. He visited 14 contiguous destitute areas and chaired 7 symposia on poverty alleviation. After 8 years of hard work, 832 impoverished counties as well as 128,000 villages have been removed from the poverty list, and nearly 100 million poor rural residents have risen above the poverty line. Overall regional poverty and extreme poverty are now things of the past. General Secretary Xi has also commanded an all-out people's war against the COVID-19 pandemic. With people's interests and lives high on the agenda, he has overseen the overall situation with resolute decision, rational guidance and composed manner, offering the underlying support to the strategic achievements of COVID-19 prevention and control.

Third, the CPC never forgets the great initiative of its internal development. It has constantly improved its organization, ideology, discipline, conduct and personnel to enhance its creativity, solidarity and productivity. The Party keeps the anti-corruption campaign going and exercises strict discipline on all fronts to always keep abreast of the times and serve as the backbone of all the Chinese people. As General Secretary Xi pointed out, "It takes a good blacksmith to make good steel. China's success hinges on the CPC, and especially on the principle that the CPC should supervise its own conduct and abide in full by the code of discipline." The CPC must initiate reform from the inside and make itself even stronger to maintain its vigor and vitality and live up to the historic mission of the new era. Since the 18th National Congress of the CPC, a number of officials across the ranks who have violated party discipline or laws have been investigated and penalized nationwide. According to the public opinion poll conducted by the National Bureau of Statistics of China, 95.8% of the respondents deemed the Party's discipline campaign effective, a 16.5% increase from 2012. *The 2020 Trust Barometer* published by Edelman, a global leading consultancy in public relations, showed that China has been topping the chart for 3 consecutive years among the world's major economies, with 90% of the population trusting its government.

Fourth, the CPC is committed to the progress of mankind. The Party believes that peace and development are the trending themes of the times. China will answer the call for peace, development and win-win cooperation, and remain committed to world peace, global development and international order. China stands ready to work with all the other countries for an open, inclusive, clean and beautiful world that features lasting peace, universal security and common prosperity. As General Secretary Xi pointed out, "The future of each and every nation and country is interlocked. We should sail in the same boat, share weal and woe, endeavor to build this planet of ours into a single harmonious family, and turn people's aspiration for a better life into reality. The CPC takes an open attitude for more exchanges in governance experience with political parties of other countries. It also welcomes dialogue with different civilizations to enhance strategic trust. China will join hands with people in all countries to build a community with a shared future and a better world!" China has extended its COVID-19 support to over 150 countries and 10 international organizations, including 220 billion masks, 2.25 billion PPEs and 1.02 billion test kits, and sent 36 medical teams to 34 countries including Ethiopia. China is also donating or will donate vaccines to 80 countries and 3 international organizations, exporting vaccines to more than 40 countries, and cooperating with more than 10 countries in vaccine research, development and manufacturing. In response to a UN appeal, we have donated vaccines to peacekeepers from various countries. We are also ready to work with the International Olympic Committee to provide vaccines to Olympians, offering our solid support to our friends in their prevention and control against the pandemic.

A good understanding of the CPC is the gateway to solid knowledge of China. As the world's largest ruling party with over 96 million members, the century-old CPC will follow the lead of its leadership and stay true to its purpose and mission. Committed to peaceful development, China will enhance its partnership with Ethiopia and other countries to step up its contribution to mankind development.

Glossary

arduous *adj.*	艰辛的,困难的
renewal *n.*	恢复,重新开始;延长;更新
dedication *n.*	奉献,献身;献词

trample *v.*	踩,踏
bramble *n.*	荆棘
thicket *n.*	灌木丛,树丛
indiscriminately *adv.*	不加选择地;任意地
contiguous *adj.*	相邻的,相接的
destitute *adj.*	贫困的,贫穷的
symposia *n.*	座谈会;专题讨论会
abide *v.*	遵守;容忍,忍受
GDP	国内生产总值(Gross Domestic Product)
Theory of Three Represents	"三个代表"重要思想
Scientific Outlook on Development	科学发展观
Xi Jinping Thought on Socialism with Chinese Characteristics for a New Era	习近平新时代中国特色社会主义思想
Four Comprehensives	"四个全面"
Omari	奥马里,摩洛哥真实性与现代党前总书记
Morocco's Authenticity and Modernity Party	摩洛哥真实性与现代党(2008年成立,众议院第二大党)
hinge on	取决于,依赖
penalize *v.*	惩处,处罚
18th National Congress of the CPC	中国共产党第十八次全国代表大会
National Bureau of Statistics of China	中国国家统计局
The 2020 Trust Barometer	《2020"信任度晴雨表"报告》
PPE	个人防护用品(Personal Protective Equipment)
test kit	检测试剂盒

Ethiopia 埃塞俄比亚

International Olympic Committee 国际奥林匹克委员会

Active Reading Tasks

Task 1　Annotate the text.

(1) Annotate the passage by highlighting key points related to the founding and mission of the Communist Party of China.

(2) Identify and annotate the key historical events and milestones in the development of the Communist Party of China from its founding in 1921 to the present day.

Task 2　Create mind maps.

(1) Give a mind map of the history of the Communist Party of China.

(2) Generate a mind map of the key principles and ideologies of the Communist Party of China.

Text B

How Does China's Whole-Process People's Democracy Work?

China aims to improve the system of institutions through which the people run the country, according to a report to the 20th National Congress of the Communist Party of China (CPC).

The section in the report on whole-process people's democracy stressed the need to strengthen the institutions through which the people run the country, fully develop consultative democracy, actively develop democracy at the primary level, and consolidate and develop the broadest possible patriotic united front.

The people will be encouraged to participate in political affairs and guarantee their ability to engage in democratic elections, consultations, decision-making, management, and oversight in accordance with the law, according to the report.

Over the years, China has sought to encourage democratic values by ensuring the right of the people to participate extensively in state governance. In 2019, the Party advanced a key concept of whole-process people's democracy in responding to people's new demands and aspirations for democracy.

China's whole-process people's democracy, with the CPC leadership as its fundamental guarantee and the people's congress system as its institutional vehicle, is combined with electoral democracy and consultative democracy, covering the economic, political, cultural, social, eco-environmental and other fields.

Chinese lawmakers are now seeking to incorporate whole-process people's democracy into the country's Legislation Law. A draft amendment to the law has been submitted to the ongoing session of the National People's Congress (NPC) Standing Committee for review on October 27.

How is whole-process people's democracy practiced?

Primarily, China's democracy works institutionally via the formal processes of the people's congresses at various levels of political organization, culminating in the NPC, which is the highest organ of state power.

With the power to enact laws, the NPC as a whole meets annually in March, and its Standing Committee meets throughout the year on the preparation work for various pieces of legislation.

The deputies to people's congresses come from all regions, ethnic groups, sectors and social groups across China, and function at national, provincial, city, county and township levels.

At the end of 2020, there were over 2.62 million people serving as deputies to people's congresses, with those at county and township levels accounting for 94.5 percent of the total.

During the first half of 2021, 2,629,447 deputies from China's 31 provinces, autonomous regions and municipalities were directly elected to the county and township-level people's congresses, with 1.064 billion voters involved in the elections.

Since the launch of reform and opening up in 1978, about 3,000 NPC deputies have gathered in the presence of Party and state leaders at the NPC session each year to discuss plans for national development and problems affecting people's livelihoods.

Also, the NPC opens its website to solicit public comments before enacting draft laws and amendments. Since 2008, opinions for over 240 draft laws have been publicly solicited online.

During the compilation of the Civil Code, the first civil code in China that covers areas like real rights, personality rights, marriage and family, and inheritance, more than 1.02 million comments were collected from 425,000 participants.

In terms of social affairs, grassroots contact stations across China have become platforms to encourage people's participation in grassroots governance and democratic practices.

For instance, workers from contact stations in Shanghai gather residents to discuss issues related to community construction, including adding lifts to old residential buildings. In 2021, Shanghai authorities set a goal of adding 1,000 lifts to old buildings. Ultimately, 1,579 were added, three times as many as in the previous decade, and a further 2,000 are planned for this year.

"We will implement the concept of whole-process people's democracy throughout all aspects of our community governance. We will build up a structure where people can discuss and decide public affairs by the most real, widespread and effective democracy... and create a better community for everyone," Dai Tao, secretary of the Party working committee in Hongqiao Subdistrict, told CGTN.

What's the origin of China's democracy?

Whole-process people's democracy refers to China's model of democracy, ensuring all major legislative decisions are formulated through democratic decision-making.

As a comprehensive and coordinated system focused on national development, social governance and people's lives, it covers a population of over 1.4 billion people from 56 ethnic groups, making sure that people's voices are heard and their wishes are represented in political and social life.

"China conceives democracy as broader, more encompassing, than free and fair multi-party elections," said Robert Lawrence Kuhn, a China political and economic analyst.

"Democracy in the Party-led system involves assessing and absorbing public opinion via feedback mechanisms at all levels of government and people's congresses, such as polling to discern what people think."

"Whole-process people's democracy is a creation of the CPC in leading the people to pursue, develop and realize democracy," according to the full text of *China: Democracy That Works* published by the State Council Information Office of China.

The concept derives from the legacy of the CPC's democratic practices. During the revolutionary era in the 1940s, the CPC adopted various methods to mobilize illiterate farmers to vote in elections. The most popular one was "bean voting", whereby villagers put beans into a bowl behind the candidate they wanted to vote for.

Democracy in China is different in terms of the procedures and format from other countries, but it keeps China very dynamic, said Victor Gao, chair professor at Soochow University in an interview with CGTN.

💡 Glossary

consolidate *v.*	使巩固,使加强;合并,统一
solicit *v.*	征求,请求
inheritance *n.*	继承物,遗产;遗传特征
formulate *v.*	规划,制定
conceive *v.*	构思,设想
procedure *n.*	程序,规程
discern *v.*	看出,觉察出;了解

illiterate *adj.*	不识字的
candidate *n.*	候选人；申请者
20th National Congress of the Communist Party of China (CPC)	中国共产党第二十次全国代表大会
Legislation Law	立法法
National People's Congress (NPC) Standing Committee	全国人民代表大会常务委员会
Civil Code	民法典
CGTN	中国国际电视台(China Global Television Network)
Robert Lawrence Kuhn	罗伯特·劳伦斯·库恩，美国库恩基金会主席、中国问题专家
State Council Information Office of China	中国国务院新闻办公室
Victor Gao	高志凯，苏州大学讲座教授、中欧联合投资有限公司副董事长、中国国际关系学会理事
Soochow University	苏州大学

Active Reading Tasks

Task 1 Analyze.

(1) Analyze how whole-process people's democracy is practiced in China, focusing on the institutional processes of the people's congresses and the role of the National People's Congress (NPC) in enacting laws and overseeing governance. Take note of the levels of political organization involved and the representation of diverse groups in the congresses.

(2) Analyze how major legislative decisions are formulated through democratic decision-making in China's political system. Consider the significance of ensuring that people's voices are heard and represented in political and social life, as highlighted in the concept of whole-process people's democracy.

Task 2　Discuss.

Victor Gao said, "Democracy in China is different in terms of the procedures and format from other countries, but it keeps China very dynamic." Do you agree? Discuss with your classmates how China's unique procedures and formats contribute to the inclusiveness and effectiveness of its governance and decision-making processes.

Voice beyond Borders

Text C

How to Precisely Convey China's Political Discourse to the West?[①]

Will the translation of "加强党的建设" into "Party building" mislead foreigners by making them think China is talking about a building where they could take children to hold their birthday party? In a situation where the Western media control the international discourse, how can we manifest China's real image and true stories, and precisely convey China's voices to the West? What might be the effective solutions to the Western media's stigmatization?

China News Service's (CNS) W. E. Talk invited honorary chief English editor of Foreign Languages Press CICG, David Ferguson, who has been editing China's political works and contributing to China's external communication for more than 10 years, to answer these questions.

Here's the excerpt of the dialogue.

CNS: As China's international influence increases, Western countries are giving greater emphasis to affairs in China, but the disappointing results are misinterpretation and misunderstanding. Why does information that China wants to convey to the West often end in misunderstanding?

David Ferguson: It's a mistake to consider it as a "misunderstanding", which suggests a problem that can be resolved by providing facts and reason. The fact is that China is being subjected to a deliberate campaign of misrepresentation and stigmatization by Western media

---

① The author of the text is David W. Ferguson, honorary chief English editor of Foreign Languages Press, recipient of the Chinese Government Friendship Award and the Special Book Award of China. He has participated in the revision and polishing of English translations of several government white papers and other key Chinese books.

and politicians, with the intent of creating hostility to China. The USA calls the shots in the Western world. The USA has been "top dog" in the world for a relatively short period of time in historical terms, but it now sees a challenger to its predominance, and as usual its first response is to lash out—to destroy a "China Threat" that only exists in its rather twisted psyche—rather than to seek partnership and accommodation. The rest of the West is simply trotting along behind USA. Some Western media create stories, not truths on China-related subjects.

China has to recognize that trying to solve the problem by "explaining things better" is no use. The people behind the campaign have no intention of allowing China to present a more balanced and accurate picture, and they have the power to block or distort information coming from the Chinese side because the international discourse is in the hands of Western media.

CNS: Some Western media tend to interpret China's political discourse in the wrong way, or even with ill intentions. What might be the effective solutions to this situation?

David Ferguson: Accepting that a deliberate campaign of misrepresentation and stigmatization by Western media and politicians is ongoing in the international arena, I think the best way for China to tackle the situation is to invest more in its informal discourse—its soft power—and to directly reach out to Western audiences.

For example, they can bypass the Western media through movies—bear in mind that a movie goes direct to its final audience without being distorted through local political and media filters. The Chinese are good at making big movies. "My People, My Country", the movie released for China's 70th Anniversary is such a clever film. China should preserve its formal political discourse as China's official voice, and at the same time it should develop its informal discourse, to engage with Western audiences on a human level.

CNS: Facing foreigners who have no idea of China's history or culture, how do we make them better understand China's political discourse? Can you please identify the problems in translating China's policies and political concepts?

David Ferguson: The most important issue in translating political discourse is not just translating words but presenting a message.

For example, we can often see the word "科学" in China's political discourse. But in most cases, it will be directly translated into "science" or "scientific". But in English, "science" refers to natural science, which is obviously not the meaning of "科学" in China's political discourse. The Scientific Outlook on Development is a perfect example of this. This represented a massive transformation in China's development strategy—a switch from purely economic growth to a balanced strategy considering economic, social, and environmental factors. But the English words chosen capture nothing of this—they make it sound like some kind of technocratic scheme involving chemistry and physics. So China missed a huge opportunity to send a vital and important message to the world about a fundamental strategic change.

China's political discourse is very conceptual and abstract in nature, so you have to deconstruct the concept and provide Western audiences with the actual meaning behind the concept. An example of good translation is Xi Jinping Thought on Socialism with Chinese Characteristics for a New Era.

Xi Jinping Thought represents a philosophy and a set of values and principles that will endure for decades. Therefore great care was given to the precise wording. Every syllable had to be weighed and optimized.

The initial formulation used the words "in the new era". However, it was felt that this suggested that the "new era" was something that was being imposed on China by external forces, and that China was reacting. After consideration by all the most senior experts in Chinese translation circles, it was agreed to use "for a new era". This implies more that China is driving and proactively controlling the development trends of the new era.

And "Party building" is one of the biggest problems. It's a very important and often-used expression, but if you say it to an English speaker who knows nothing about China's discourse, their first reaction will be that you are talking about a building where you take children to hold their birthday party. Thus it should be translated as "strengthening the Party".

CNS: When conveying China's political to the West, how can we make China's discourse into an international discourse? When translating China's policies and political concepts, what will cause misunderstandings among Western audiences? And how can we avoid them?

David Ferguson: English is the international language, so China has to make its discourse understandable in English. 80 years ago Chairman Mao made a speech during the Yan'an Rectification—which he called *Oppose Stereotyped Party Writing*—in which he criticized the Party's writing style.

Then in 2005, when he was the Party Secretary of Zhejiang, President Xi wrote an article detailing similar criticisms, and warning against issues like repetition, verbosity, clichés, and formulaic writing.

China has to adopt these counsels when conveying its political discourse to foreigners.

Things like the Two Upholds, the Three Represents, the Four Confidences, etc. may confuse the Western public which therefore has no idea of their importance and what is behind them.

We need a completely new approach that starts by recognizing that there's a problem. We need to stop fussing about whether something is "the same as the Chinese" and start looking to create a message that is understandable. The best way to do that is to ask yourself the question "How would a native English speaker express this?" rather than "How can we translate this Chinese?"

CNS: If we say, translation is a cross-cultural process, can conveyance of China's political discourse somehow correct Western preconceptions towards China?

David Ferguson: In my view it is an issue of culture not translation. But I think translators and interpreters should play a far more active role in the process of conveying China's political discourse.

Creativity has to play a greater role in political translation than other translations, because political discourse is dry in nature and hard to understand, so translators and interpreters should learn to not only translate the words but also analyze the message and even make some adaptations. This is one way to correct Western preconceptions towards China, which are a result of Western media misinterpretation and stigmatization.

Glossary

stigmatization *n.*	侮辱,谴责
predominance *n.*	优势;卓越
technocratic *adj.*	技术专家治国论的;技术专家政治论的
syllable *n.*	音节,发音
cliché *n.*	陈腔滥调
preconception *n.*	偏见;先入之见
misinterpretation *n.*	误解,错误解释
China News Service	中国新闻社
W. E. Talk	东西问·中外对话
Foreign Languages Press	外文出版社

CICG	中国外文出版发行事业局（China International Communications Group）
Scientific Outlook on Development	科学发展观
Xi Jinping Thought on Socialism with Chinese Characteristics for a New Era	习近平新时代中国特色社会主义思想
Yan'an Rectification	延安整风运动
Oppose Stereotyped Party Writing	《反对党八股》
Two Upholds	"两个维护"
Three Represents	"三个代表"
Four Confidences	"四个自信"

Active Reading Tasks

Task 1 Answer questions.

(1) What are the reasons behind the misinterpretation and stigmatization of China's political discourse by Western media and politicians? What is the impact of deliberate campaigns aimed at creating hostility towards China and the role of the USA in shaping the international discourse?

(2) Is it important to invest in informal discourse, such as movies, to bypass Western media filters and engage with Western audiences on a human level, why?

(3) Is there a need for a new approach that focuses on creating messages that are easily understandable in English?

Task 2 Discuss.

Analyze the role of translators and interpreters in correcting Western preconceptions towards China through the conveyance of China's political discourse. Discuss with your classmates the challenges faced by translators in accurately capturing the conceptual and abstract nature of China's political concepts for Western audiences. How can creativity and adaptation in political translation help in addressing misinterpretations and creating a more balanced and accurate portrayal of China's policies and values in the international arena?

Practical Assignment

1. Contact an expert or individual with expertise in CPC's history, leadership and impact on China's domestic and international affairs. Develop a set of interview questions focusing on the historical evolution of the CPC, or the CPC's commitment to its original aspiration and mission, or its contributions to China's development and global engagement. Analyze the perspective gathered from the interview, and prepare a presentation or report summarizing the key findings from the interview.

2. Watch the videos provided in the section of "Additional Resources", and reflect on the CPC's commitment to exploring a development path aligned with China's realities, its fundamental stance of siding with the people, its internal development initiatives. Then facilitate a group discussion or seminar to engage in a critical analysis of the CPC's historical journey, its leadership, and contributions to global peace and development.

Additional Resources

Digital Resource 1-1

Unit 2

Economy

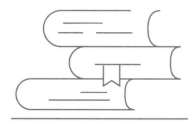

二十大报告选摘

Report to the 20th National Congress of the Communist Party of China (Excerpt)

中国坚持对外开放的基本国策,坚定奉行互利共赢的开放战略,不断以中国新发展为世界提供新机遇,推动建设开放型世界经济,更好惠及各国人民。中国坚持经济全球化正确方向,推动贸易和投资自由化便利化,推进双边、区域和多边合作,促进国际宏观经济政策协调,共同营造有利于发展的国际环境,共同培育全球发展新动能,反对保护主义,反对"筑墙设垒"、"脱钩断链",反对单边制裁、极限施压。中国愿加大对全球发展合作的资源投入,致力于缩小南北差距,坚定支持和帮助广大发展中国家加快发展。

China is committed to its fundamental national policy of opening to the outside world and pursues a mutually beneficial strategy of opening up. It strives to create new opportunities for the world with its own development and to contribute its share to building an open global economy that delivers greater benefits to all peoples. China adheres to the right course of economic globalization. It strives to promote trade and investment liberalization and facilitation, advance bilateral, regional, and multilateral cooperation, and boost international macroeconomic policy coordination. It is committed to working with other countries to foster an international environment conducive to development and create new drivers for global growth. China opposes protectionism, the erection of "fences and barriers," decoupling, disruption of industrial and supply chains, unilateral sanctions, and maximum-pressure tactics. China is prepared to invest more resources in global development cooperation. It is committed to narrowing the North-South gap and supporting and assisting other developing countries in accelerating development.

Critical Reading Skill—Analytical Reading

What is analytical reading and why is it important for critical reading?

Analytical reading refers to the process of carefully examining and interpreting a text to understand its deeper meanings, structure, and components. It can only be achieved by readers with a high degree of proficiency in reading. It is known that the only way to become a proficient reader is through text analysis, and the higher the proficiency level of the reader, the more accurate the analysis will be. Analytical reading is important because it enables you to gain a profound understanding of the text, fostering critical thinking and deeper engagement with the material. By going beyond mere comprehension, analytical reading encourages you to evaluate arguments, identify underlying assumptions, and discern the significance of various elements within the text. By dissecting the structure, style, and content, you can appreciate the nuances and complexities of the material, leading to more informed and thoughtful interpretations. Moreover, it enhances your ability to synthesize information from multiple sources, supports effective communication of ideas, and develops essential skills for academic and professional success.

Tips to train and develop analytical reading skill:

Analytical reading is the mechanism for being a demanding reader and is the "ideal performance" of a reader. To train and develop the skill, you can employ the following tips.

(1) Read closely. Read carefully and pay attention to the details. Figure out what the whole text is about. List the major parts in their order and relation to one another and outline these parts to outline the whole text. Define the problem or problems the author has tried to solve. When you encounter a difficult text or paragraph, slow down, re-read it, and pause until you can summarize for yourself in 1-2 sentences.

(2) Interpret. Interpret the key words and grasp the author's leading arguments by examining the most important sentences. Know the author's arguments by finding them in

sequences of sentences or constructing them out of sequences of sentences. Determine which problems the author has solved, and which the author has not.

(3)Criticize. Do not say you agree, disagree, or suspend judgement, until you can say "I understand the text". Demonstrate that you recognize the difference between knowledge and mere opinion by presenting good reasons for any critical judgement you make. If you disagree, show where the author is uninformed, or where the author is misinformed, or where the author is illogical or where the author's analysis or account is incomplete.

Warm-up Questions

1. When it comes to reform and opening up, what do you think of?
2. Do you know any of China's current economic achievements?
3. What are the primary factors that contribute to China's economic growth?

Text

The Reason Why China's Economy Created a Miracle in Nearly 40 Years of Reform and Opening Up

    2018 marks the 40th anniversary of the reform and opening up. I believe that for us, the 40th anniversary is very important and worth-celebrating. I often say that I am the sixth generation intellectual who has been striving for the great rejuvenation of the Chinese nation since the Opium War. The first generation, as we all know, is the one that promoted the Self-Strengthening Movement, represented by Zeng Guofan and Li Hongzhang. The second generation includes Kang Youwei, Liang Qichao, and Sun Yat-sen, who promoted the Hundred Days' Reform and the democratic revolution. The third generation comprises figures like Chen Duxiu, Li Dazhao, and Hu Shi, who advocated the New Culture Movement and the May Fourth Movement. The fourth generation refers to those who graduated from universities after the May Fourth Movement, participating in socialist revolution and the War of Resistance against Japanese Aggression. The fifth generation refers to people who entered university after the founding of the People's Republic of China in 1949, and then engaged in socialist construction after graduation. The sixth generation, to which I belong, entered university after the resumption of the college entrance examination in 1977 and 1978, and then participated in the reform and opening up after graduation.

    Compared with the previous five generations of intellectuals, we are the luckiest. As mentioned in President Xi's report to the 19th National Congress, we are closer to, more confident, and capable of achieving the great rejuvenation of the Chinese nation than the previous generations. The main reason for such confidence is the contribution made during the nearly 40 years of reform and opening up. I would like to reflect on our past hardships and joys. After the efforts of the previous five generations, what was the situation in China at the beginning of the reform and opening up in 1978? At that time, the per capita GDP was only 381 yuan. It is known that the poorest place in the world was the sub-Saharan African countries, where the average per capita GDP surpassed China's. Our exports and imports accounted for only 9.7% of our GDP, meaning that more than 90% of our GDP was not related to the international economy. At that time, over 80% of the population lived in rural areas, and 84% of the people lived below the international poverty line of $1.25 a day.

However, from 1978 to 2016, the average annual GDP growth rate reached 9.5% over 38 years. It can be said that in human history, there has never been a precedent of such a high growth rate lasting for such a long time, especially in a country with such a large population and such a poor foundation. Therefore, it is very appropriate to call the 40 years of reform and opening up a miracle for China.

After 38 years of high-speed growth, the GDP increased by 33.5 times, and our per capita GDP reached 53,980 yuan in 2016. Our country's total economic output accounted for a larger share of the world economy. In terms of market exchange rates, in 1978, we only accounted for 2.3% of the world's GDP; last year, our GDP reached 14.9%. During this period, the economic growth was very fast, and the pace of opening up to the outside world was also very rapid. By measuring trade growth, from 1978 to 2016, our average annual trade growth rate was 14.5%. With such rapid growth, we are now the world's second largest economy, according to market exchange rates. If measured by purchasing power parity, we are already the world's largest economy.

We are also the world's largest trading nation, making a significant contribution to global poverty reduction efforts. Over the past 40 years (1978-2018), 70% of the reduction in global poverty has come from China. If the poverty population in China is excluded, the global poverty population has not only failed to decrease but has also increased. Moreover, we are the only market economy that has not experienced a financial crisis.

It is precisely because of the achievements of the nearly 40 years of reform and opening up that we can say that we are now closer to, more confident, and capable of achieving the great rejuvenation of the Chinese nation than at any other time in history.

How did the reform and opening up create the Chinese miracle?

Since the reform and opening up, our economic scale has increased a lot. The real growth is achievable only by continuously improving labor productivity levels.

How do we achieve a continuous increase in labor productivity? Firstly, companies need to constantly innovate in technology, enabling every worker to produce more and better products. Secondly, companies need to continually transform and upgrade, shifting labor, resources, and capital from industries with lower added value to those with higher added value.

We know that agriculture has a relatively low added value, while manufacturing has a higher added value. By transferring a large amount of rural labor to urban manufacturing, an adjustment in industrial structure is achieved. These are the two mechanisms for upgrading the industrial structure, continuously improving the skill level of labor force, and increasing income.

The two mechanisms are the same for developed countries and developing countries, and they are both fair. However, there is one difference. Since the Industrial Revolution, developed countries have always been technologically ahead of the world; the value added by their industries has always been leading. Their technology and industries are at the forefront of international technology and industry. Developed countries have a very stable economic growth rate through technological innovation, which is about 2% every year. If factor like population growth is considered, the growth rate for developed countries has been about 2% annually over the past 100 years. For developing countries, as not technologically advanced as we are, technological innovation means using better technology than the current technology for commodity production. Industrial upgrade means entering an industry with higher value added than the current industry, not necessarily requiring new inventions.

This possibility is referred to in economics as the advantage of latecomers. In terms of technological innovation and industrial upgrade, developing countries have an advantage compared to developed countries.

If we use the method of introduction, the cost will be lower than inventing by ourselves, and the risk will also be much lower. If developing countries know how to utilize the advantage of latecomers, the speed of economic growth will be higher than that of developed countries. But how much higher? Theoretically, only slightly higher. From the experience perspective, after the Second World War, 13 out of over 200 economies experienced accelerated economic growth, achieving a growth rate of 7% or higher annually, sustaining rapid economic growth for 25 years. Since the reform and opening up, we have become one of these 13 economies.

Why were we able to maintain stable and high-speed growth after the reform and opening up? The main reason is that at that time, we did not simply copy foreign theories.

Taking the large state-owned enterprises at that time as an example, since they could not survive without subsidies, we decided to make a transition possible. At the same time, we opened up market access for labor-intensive industries where we had a comparative advantage; we also attracted foreign investment. In the beginning, the national infrastructure was very poor. To transform the industries with comparative advantages into competitive advantages, it was necessary to build good infrastructure. Since there was no capacity to build the national infrastructure, we started with special economic zones. Through this pragmatic approach, rapid development ensued, and the comparative advantage was turned into a competitive advantage. This led to a significant increase in exports and profits, resulting in an average 9% economic growth rate over 38 consecutive years.

While achieving stable and rapid development, we also accumulated capital, gradually transforming from an economy with a capital shortage to one with an abundant capital. Subsidies were a lifeline during the stage of comparative advantage, but now that we have achieved comparative advantage, the enterprises have the ability to sustain themselves. Providing subsidies at this stage would be like adding flowers to brocade—unnecessary. Therefore, the Third Plenary Session of the 18th CPC Central Committee proposed comprehensive deepening reform. We can cancel those protectionist subsidies left over from the transition period and establish a sound market economy system. I believe this is the reason why we have been able to achieve rapid development after the reform and opening up, while other transitional countries experienced economic collapse, stagnation, and continuous crises.

What are the Chinese lessons behind the economic miracle?

Based on this reflection and review, I believe that we can learn some valuable lessons for our future development.

For the economy to develop successfully, it must leverage its comparative advantages to establish competitive advantages. Our labor productivity is still significantly lower than that of developed countries like the United States, indicating that there is still a lot of untapped advantage due to our latecomer status. We are able to maintain a medium to high growth rate, which is still considered high growth in the global context. I believe this situation will not change in the short term, but the premise is that we must leverage our comparative advantages to establish competitive advantages.

During our transition since the reform and opening up, there is a lesson we must remember, and that is the need to emancipate our minds and seek truth from facts. As a developing and transitioning country, we have many distortions, interventions, and loopholes. However, these are all for a reason. We cannot just follow textbooks; we must liberate our minds, seek truth from facts, and continuously explore and practice. Practice has no end, and theoretical innovation has no end either.

The conditions of a developing country like China are relatively similar to those of other developing countries. The theories proposed based on China's experience will undoubtedly serve as valuable reference for other developing countries. The Chinese nation is pursuing great rejuvenation, and all developing countries share our dream of becoming modern and industrialized nations. For them, China's experience holds better reference value than the experience and theories of developed countries. Perhaps we can look forward to the arrival of a new era and a new world where "one hundred flowers in full blossom brings spring to the garden".

💡 Glossary

Hundred Days' Reform	百日维新
rejuvenation *n.*	复兴
purchasing power parity	购买力平价(PPP),是根据各国不同的价格水平计算出来的货币之间的等值系数,目的是对各国的国内生产总值进行合理比较
labor productivity	劳动生产率
added value	附加值
leverage *v.*	发挥杠杆作用
subsidy *n.*	补贴
consecutive *adj.*	连续的
Third Plenary Session of the Eighteenth Central Committee	十八届三中全会
untapped *adj.*	未开发的
emancipate *v.*	解放
loophole *n.*	漏洞
usher *v.*	开创

Analytical Reading Tasks

Task 1 Answer questions.

(1) Can you summarize the main idea of the author's speech within 5 sentences?

(2) What are the major details the author employed to support his arguments?

(3) According to the author, what are the Chinese lessons behind our economic miracle? Is there anything missing in his summary of the lessons in your opinion, and why do you think so?

Task 2 Discuss.

In the last paragraph, the author says, "The conditions of a developing country like China are relatively similar to those of other developing countries. The theories proposed based on China's experience will undoubtedly serve as valuable reference for other developing countries." Do you agree? Discuss with your classmates and see whether your answers are different.

Text B

China's Miraculous Achievements in Numbers

From 1921 to 2021, the Communist Party of China has led the country to create countless miracles. As China's overall national strength continues growing, the country has become the biggest engine to drive global economic growth.

China has become a mainstay of global economic growth

China has been the world's second largest economy for 11 consecutive years from 2010.

China's GDP reached almost 101.3 trillion yuan in 2020, up 2.2 percent from a year earlier, making the country the only major economy in the world with positive growth. The GDP figure represented an increase of 1,500 times from 1952.

With a commitment to supply-side structural reform, China's economic structure has continued to improve, and new dynamism has been unleashed. In the past several years, the tertiary industry, mainly including finance as well as science and technology, has steadily increased its contribution to China's GDP, and become a pillar industry of the national economy.

Foreign trade develops steadily and rapidly

From 1948 to 2020, China's total foreign trade volume surged from $907 billion to $4.65 trillion with an average annual growth rate of nearly 14 percent.

The country's total imports and exports of goods expanded 1.9 percent on a yearly basis in 2020, making China the world's only major economy to register positive growth amid the pandemic, which hurt global businesses.

In 2017, China's trade volume jumped to the first spot in the world from the 26th spot in 1978, and has remained No. 1 for four years in a row up to 2020. Currently, the country has become the world's largest exporter and second-largest importer.

China's import and export trade has made a huge contribution to the world. In 2020, the country contributed 13.13 percent to the world's import and export trade volume, with the contribution growing 12 percentage points over 1948. Moreover, China's export contribution to the world surpassed 10 percent for 11 consecutive years, with the figure reaching a record high of nearly 15 percent in 2020.

Now, China's exports are shifting from low-end to high-end in the value chain.

Chinese people's per capita disposable income increased more than a hundredfold

Before 1986, the per capita disposable income of urban residents in China was less than 1,000 yuan. In 2005, the figure exceeded 10,000 yuan for the first time.

In 2020, the per capita disposable income grew by 2.1 percent year-on-year in real terms to 32,189 yuan, with the per capita disposable income of rural residents at 17,131 yuan, and at 43,834 yuan for urban residents. The per capita disposable income of urban residents surged more than a hundred times from 343.4 yuan in 1978.

China is among the countries with a relatively complete academic system

The number of scientific and technical personnel jumped from less than 50,000 in the early days of the founding of the People's Republic of China to over 5 million—the most in the world—in 2020.

In 2019, China surpassed the United States as the top source of international patent applications filed with the World Intellectual Property Organization, and it stayed ahead with 68,720 applications in 2020.

The country's total expenditures on research and development in 2020 surpassed 2.4 trillion yuan, up 180 times over the 13 billion yuan in 1980.

Spending on basic research in 2020 has nearly doubled that of 2015 and will likely exceed 150 billion yuan in 2020. During the 13th Five-Year Plan period (2016-2020), spending on basic research achieved an overall growth rate of 16.9 percent.

The contribution rate of scientific and technological progress is projected to reach 60 percent in 2020, and the proportion of the scientifically literate Chinese population has surpassed 10 percent.

In 2005, China surpassed the US to become the world's largest exporter in high-technology. By the end of 2019, the value of high-technology exports exceeded $700 billion, a figure 4.6 times that of the US, 6.88 times that of Japan and 9.16 times that of the UK.

China has realized the transformation from a country of population to a country of human resources

In the early days of the founding of the People's Republic of China, 80 percent of Chinese people were illiterate, and the average amount of schooling was only 1.6 years. Moreover, the country only had 205 institutions of higher learning with less than 120,000 students in 1949, and the gross enrollment rate was only 0.26 percent. By 2020, the average amount of schooling rose to 10.8 years.

The net enrollment rate of primary schools nationwide increased from 20 percent in 1949 to 99.96 percent in 2020, and the gross enrollment rate of China's higher education rose from 0.26 percent in 1949 to 54.4 percent in 2020.

By the end of 2020, the number of general institutes of higher education reached 2,738 with 32.85 million students on campus, taking the first spot in the world.

China became Asia's largest stock market from 2015

The number of listed companies on A-share market reached 4,373, with the total market value hitting 93.75 trillion yuan. The average annual growth of the number of listed companies and the total market value has increased 31.32 percent and 24.3 percent, respectively from 1990.

With China's economic power rising, more Chinese companies are making a splash in the global market

China had more Fortune Global 500 companies than the United States for the first time in 2020, with 133 firms on the list.

China's fruits of economic development benefit all the people in the country

China has built the world's largest social security system in the 13th Five-Year Plan period (2016-2020). The coverage rate of China's basic medical insurance program remained stable, covering more than 95 percent of the country's population by the end of 2020.

Since the beginning of reform and opening up, China has lifted 770 million impoverished rural citizens out of poverty, accounting for more than 70 percent of the world's total while also meeting the goal of ending poverty, as established in the UN *2030 Agenda for Sustainable Development*, 10 years ahead of schedule.

In 2019, the average life expectancy of the Chinese people has increased to 77.3 years, up from just 35 years when the People's Republic of China was founded.

China's transportation development turns country into strong power

China's total train mileage in operation hit 146,000 kilometers by the end of 2020, and highways registered 5.2 million kilometers, expanding by seven and 64 times respectively compared to the early period of New China.

From 2016 to 2020, the nation continued to expand the network, with the length of high-speed lines nearly doubling to 37,900 km and bullet trains handling 9 billion passenger trips.

Road networks have been further improved, with wider coverage around the country. The country's expressway mileage took the first spot globally, with 161,000 km in operation by the end of last year.

As waterway transportation grows more mature, there were 22,142 production berths at ports in China by the end of 2020, among which 2,592 were over the 10,000-ton class, accounting for 11.7 percent of the total and ranking first in the world.

Glossary

supply-side structural reform	供给侧结构性改革（一种通过调整和优化经济供给结构来推动经济发展和结构调整的改革策略）
tertiary industry	第三产业
disposable income	可支配收入
expenditure *n.*	支出
mileage *n.*	里程

Analytical Reading Tasks

Task 1 Answer questions.

(1) What achievements are listed in this text, and is there logic among the achievements?

(2) What is the main idea of the text? And is there sufficient evidence to support the main idea?

(3) If you are going to talk about China's economic achievements, will you use numbers, why?

Task 2 Make a video.

Choose one of the above-mentioned achievements and create a video highlighting China's economic changes. You can work on this project independently or collaborate with classmates, friends, or family members. Be creative, and make sure to illustrate the achievement with real-life examples and compelling stories from your surroundings.

Seven Segments Shaping China's Consumption Landscape[①]

The sheer scale of China's consumer markets continues to matter. China offers a $5 trillion consumption growth opportunity over the next decade, according to new research from the McKinsey Global Institute. Incomes are rising at pace. Consider households in the upper middle income and above (with annual incomes of $22,000 or more in 2011 international dollars, purchasing power parity basis). Today, China is home to fewer of these households than Europe. In just ten years, China could almost account for as many as Europe and the United States combined at about 400 million (Exhibit 1).

But a new chapter is being written that goes beyond scale and rising incomes. A combination of demographic and social change, and the inexorable penetration of digital technologies is reinforcing the diversity of these markets, prompting changing consumer preferences and behavior in sometimes surprising ways. How well do we know China's consumers? Let's look at some of them (Exhibit 2).

The online senior

The over-60s are expected to account for around one-quarter of China's population by 2030, an increase in the number of seniors of as much as 45 percent. Their consumption is

---

① This text was edited by Janet Bush, an MGI senior editor in the London office, and was issued on July 22, 2021. The authors are Daniel Zipser, a McKinsey & Company senior partner in Shenzhen and leader of McKinsey's Consumer & Retail Practice in Greater China; Jeongmin Seong, a McKinsey & Company partner in Shanghai and leader of the McKinsey Global Institute; and Lola Woetzel, a McKinsey & Company senior partner in Shanghai and a director of the McKinsey Global Institute.

Over the next decade the number of upper-middle income and above households in China is expected to grow by almost 70%

of households in upper-middle income and above, million
(with annual incomes of $22,000 or more in 2011 international $ purchasing power parity)

■ 2020
■ 2030

China: 235 (2020), 395 (2030), +68%
United States: 119 (2020), 126 (2030)
Europe: 268 (2020), 293 (2030)

Note: Projections based on McKinsey's baseline scenario, which assumes that China, the US and Europe's long-term growth trajectory is not materially affected by the pandemic. Growth outcomes will depend on the shape of the recovery from the pandemic and other macroeconomic factors in different geographies.
Source: McKinsey Global Institute analysis

McKinsey & Company

Exhibit 1

Seven consumers driving growth in China

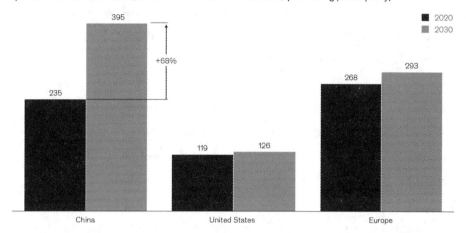

Domestic tourists
During China's May Labor Day holiday in 2021, domestic travel rebounded, and was 3% higher than in 2019; 19% of household consumption could come from travel and communication in 2030, 6 percentage points higher than in 2020

Clustered consumers
Urban areas account for 90% of GDP growth. 15+ urban clusters could amount to a majority of consumption growth.

Sharing consumers
> 60% of consumers in large cities regularly use apps selling used goods

Eco-shoppers
80% consumers are willing to pay extra for more sustainable alternatives

Online seniors
Senior consumption is expected to increase 50% 2020–2030; more than 2/3 of seniors are expected to be online

Single householders
15% of households are single-person ones today; China today has more than 240 million single adults

Digital natives
>40% of digital natives buy products spontaneously on the go, higher than in Australia, Japan, or South Korea; 50% of consumers taking out consumer loans are younger than 30, and debt is driving additional online consumption

Source: McKinsey Global Institute analysis

McKinsey & Company

Exhibit 2

expected to grow by about 150 percent during this period, twice as fast as overall consumption growth in China. The aging of China's population, and consumption opportunities, are well appreciated by many companies and investors.

However, the seniors market is changing, notably because so many of the older age group are now active online. In China, a minimum of two-thirds of seniors are expected to be online by 2030. Because so many elderly were housebound during the pandemic, this trend has accelerated.

By the end of 2020, China's over 60s accounted for more than 11 percent of the country's Internet users, almost doubling their share in only nine months. Ali Research reported that the number of seniors' monthly average users of one of the largest e-commerce platforms in China grew year-on-year about 30 percentage points faster than other age groups in 2020.

Chinese technology companies are increasingly adjusting their offerings to seniors to tap into their embrace of digital. The largest ridesharing and e-commerce platforms have all created tailored versions of their apps with increased support functions and better accessibility. However, companies and investors seeking to tap into this vibrant seniors market will need to assess the large inequality that still abounds in the senior segment.

Around 25 million seniors in China have relatively higher incomes, living on more than $50 a day (2011 international dollars, purchasing power parity basis) and will drive consumption growth in categories such as health, housing (including specialized assisted-living facilities), and leisure. However, almost double that figure—over 48 million seniors—may live on less than $11 a day (2011 international dollars, purchasing power parity basis) in 2030, and have difficulty making ends meet.

The single householder

Demographic trends have a significant influence on China's consumption landscape. China's total fertility rate continues to fall, from 1.6 in 2000 to 1.3 in 2020. In 2020, there were 12 million births, compared with 18 million births in 2000—a drop of 32 percent that left China's birth rate at its lowest level in 60 years. This is one factor behind shrinkage in the size of its average household by almost 30 percent from 3.6 people in 1999 to 2.6 people in the latest census.

But there are social changes, too. Over the past 30 years, the age at which people get married and also the age at which they have children have increased by three years. Even before the new census results, the United Nations projected that the number of under 15s could shrink from 18 percent of the total population to 16 percent in the next decade.

Not only is the size of the average household shrinking, but the single-person household is becoming ever more prominent. Today, more than 15 percent of Chinese households are single-person ones, more than double the share in 1999. The number of single adults has now topped 240 million, and they are driving a robust singles economy.

Reflecting the rising prevalence of single people, for instance, pet ownership in China has more than doubled in just five years. Catering for people exercising and even entertaining themselves alone, in China there are now one-person gym modules and mini karaoke booths.

A growing number of companies are now even exploring the potential for products and services that offer companionship, human or otherwise. For example, an "AI companion" Chatbot has already reached hundreds of millions of users, many of them single people.

The digital native

So-called "digital natives" born between 1980 and 2012 and including members of Generation Z and Millennials already account for over one-third of Asia's consumption. Twenty-nine percent of Gen Zers in China spend more than six hours a day on their mobile phones, voraciously consuming video content.

They are also spontaneous buyers—more than 40 percent of China's digital natives buy products on the go, compared with 20 to 30 percent in Australia, Japan, and Republic of Korea. Members of this generation are generally optimistic about their financial future.

In a McKinsey survey of Gen Z consumers conducted before the pandemic in October 2019, 87 percent of respondents from China said that they "felt very confident that I will be able to meet my financial goals for the life I want." This was one of the highest readings within Asia.

That confidence appears to be reflected in a willingness to borrow to finance consumption. In the same McKinsey survey, 53 percent of Chinese respondents agreed with the statement, "I buy what I want and need, even if it means I have to do it on credit." In China, half of all consumers taking out consumer loans are younger than 30 and are driving additional online consumption in categories such as apparel and consumer goods.

The eco-shopper

Asia is on the front line of climate risk, accounting for two-thirds of the global risk of economic disruption emanating from changes in the natural world. Concern is rising in Asia.

In an Ipsos poll conducted in late 2019, 85 percent of Chinese respondents said that they had made changes to the products and services they buy because they were concerned about climate change, the fourth highest reading out of 28 countries surveyed. Rising concern about the environment is translating into a rising willingness to pay for more sustainable products and packaging.

In a recent McKinsey survey, more than 80 percent of Chinese respondents, the most of any country polled, expressed willingness to pay for sustainable packaging. Concern about the environment is fueling "green" shopping preferences. A leading e-commerce player reported that the volume of green purchases on its platform has risen as much as 70 percent in 2017, with local Chinese local brands accounting for more than 85 percent of such sales.

Although sustainable alternatives are more expensive—exceeding 30 percent more in some categories, two factors are propelling the rise in green consumption. First, rising incomes are closing the gap between willingness to pay and price premiums.

Second, companies are finding innovative ways of reducing the price of green goods. For instance, a Chinese made electric vehicle (EV) costs only around $5,000, making it one of the best-selling electric vehicles in the world (although most revenue comes from domestic sales).

The sharing consumer

Economic pressures, changing consumer attitudes, and technology have combined to prompt many Asian consumers to consider alternatives to traditional ownership of goods in order to fulfill their needs. The rental and subscription economies are gaining traction in, for instance, mobility, where ridesharing is growing quickly across Asia; housing, reflecting the fact that some of the most expensive property cities on a price-to-income basis are in China; and electronics.

Consumers are also embracing secondhand ownership. China's used or preowned goods market from cars to items of clothing has doubled since 2016 to $145 billion. According to QuestMobile, it is estimated that more than 60 percent of consumers in China's largest cities regularly using apps selling used goods. The largest secondhand goods e-commerce platforms had more than 30 million sellers and doubled its gross merchandise value in 2020.

Another increasingly pervasive shift is toward ownership of digital, rather than physical, goods and services. For all these shifts, consumers in China still remain likely to own more, rather than less, in the future, as incomes continue to expand.

The clustered consumer

About 90 percent of consumption growth in China is expected to take place in cities given continuing urbanization. China's megacities are set to experience growth in their high-income households. Shanghai alone is expected to add about 3 million high-income households, not far short of the 3.2 million increase expected in the whole of Japan.

But the story about urban consumption is not restricted to megacities. So-called middleweight cities are growing 2 percentage points faster than the 50 largest cities in Asia. Increasingly, companies will also need to understand how cities interact with each other.

Chinese cities can be grouped into different clusters based on their similarities in terms of consumer behavior, geographic proximity, and infrastructure network. The government of China's plan to connect urban clusters with railway and road networks could facilitate consumption growth within and across different clusters. Companies can develop tailored strategies for 15+ clusters and adjust their go-to-market approach.

The domestic tourist

As incomes rise, spending on discretionary categories will increase. Travel and communication now accounts for 16 percent of household consumption, up from 13 percent in 2010. It is expected to rise to 19 percent by 2030. China's tourism industry was thriving before the pandemic.

The number of domestic trips grew from 2.1 billion in 2010 to over 6 billion in 2019 while international travel expanded from 52 million to about 160 million. The pandemic inevitably reduced international travel to almost zero and even domestic tourism by almost half during 2020. However, while the effects on international travel still linger, domestic travel has fully recovered and even outperformed 2019. There are multiple signs of a bounce back in tourism.

During 2021's Labor Day, domestic trips were up 3 percent from the same day in 2019. Reservations via China's largest online travel agency Ctrip were up 30 percent year-on-year, and hotel average occupancy bounced back to 2019 levels. These gains partly reflect the waning of the impact on people's lives of the pandemic in China, but also the fact that many companies engaged in tourism and travel have made strenuous efforts to overcome caution due to the pandemic and tap into latent demand.

For instance, 7 Days Inn launched "safe stay" activity, offering discounts and implementing strict standards for disinfection during the 2021 Chinese New Year, while Air China provided eligible passengers with free refunds and rescheduling services.

Some regional companies were able to recover sales in advance of recovery across the rest of the economy. For example, Hainan's duty free sales in particular more than doubled in 2020. A new McKinsey survey of attitudes among Chinese tourists reveals short-term concerns, but continued positivity about long-term domestic travel (outdoor scenic trips are the most popular, followed by beach or resort holidays).

The sheer scale of China's consumer markets and rising incomes remain key considerations for consumer-facing companies, but they need to move beyond these lenses and track, understand, and learn how to serve markets that are changing radically—socially, demographically, and technologically. They will need to refine strategy to take account not only of income levels, but also new channels and new behavior even within their established customer bases.

Glossary

McKinsey Global Institute	麦肯锡全球研究所
inexorable *adj.*	不可阻挡的
Ali Research	阿里研究
ridesharing *n.*	拼车服务
Generation Z	Z世代,指于1995—2009年出生的一代人,通常被称为千禧一代的后续世代,这一代人以数字化技术的普及和互联网的发展为特征
Millennials *n.*	千禧一代,是指出生于20世纪,在跨入21世纪(2000年)后才成年的一代人,这代人的成长阶段几乎与互联网的高速发展时期相吻合
emanate *v.*	源自
gross merchandise value	商品交易总额
infrastructure *n.*	基础设施
tailored *adj.*	定制的
discretionary *adj.*	自主的,可选的,自行决定的
strenuous *adj.*	艰苦的

Analytical Reading Tasks

Task 1   Answer questions.

(1) What is the McKinsey Global Institute? Is their analysis of China's consumer markets reliable, why?

(2) What is the purpose of the report?

(3) According to the text, what contribute to the diversity of China's consumer markets? Are there any other important factors not included?

(4) Are the seven consumption segments interrelated? If so, how? If not, why?

(5) If you are planning to start your own business after graduation, do you think this report is helpful for you, if yes, in what way is it helpful?

Task 2   Discuss.

Given the projected growth and diversity of China's consumer markets, what strategic approaches should companies adopt to effectively cater to the distinct needs and preferences of different consumer segments, such as seniors, single households, digital natives, eco-shoppers, sharing consumers, clustered consumers, and domestic tourists? Discuss with your classmates the potential challenges and opportunities the seven segments present for businesses.

Conduct a survey.

In the daily lives of ordinary people, income is an important indicator of the country's economic development. Have you noticed the income differences across different generations? Have you thought about the reasons behind the differences? Please conduct a survey on the income history of a family spanning three generations. Gather data including the selection criteria for families, the time-frame covered (years/decades), and employ various methods such as interviews, documentation review, and filming to capture comprehensive findings. This survey aims to illuminate changes and trends in China's family income over time. Share your findings with the class to foster a deeper understanding of how China's economic circumstances evolve across generations.

Digital Resource 2-1

Unit 3

Diplomacy

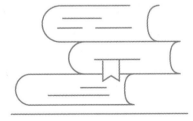

二十大报告选摘

Report to the 20th National Congress of the Communist Party of China (Excerpt)

我们全面推进中国特色大国外交,推动构建人类命运共同体,坚定维护国际公平正义,倡导践行真正的多边主义,旗帜鲜明反对一切霸权主义和强权政治,毫不动摇反对任何单边主义、保护主义、霸凌行径。我们完善外交总体布局,积极建设覆盖全球的伙伴关系网络,推动构建新型国际关系。我们展现负责任大国担当,积极参与全球治理体系改革和建设,全面开展抗击新冠肺炎疫情国际合作,赢得广泛国际赞誉,我国国际影响力、感召力、塑造力显著提升。

We have pursued major-country diplomacy with Chinese characteristics on all fronts. We have promoted the development of a human community with a shared future and stood firm in protecting international fairness and justice. We have advocated and practiced true multilateralism. We have taken a clear-cut stance against hegemonism and power politics in all their forms, and we have never wavered in our opposition to unilateralism, protectionism, and bullying of any kind. We have improved China's overall diplomatic agenda and worked actively to build a global network of partnerships and foster a new type of international relations. We have demonstrated China's sense of duty as a responsible major country, actively participating in the reform and development of the global governance system and engaging in all-around international cooperation in the fight against COVID-19. All this has seen us win widespread international recognition. China's international influence, appeal, and power to shape have risen markedly.

Critical Reading Skill—Evaluation

Why evaluation is important for critical reading?

In critical reading, "evaluation" refers to the process of assessing a text's arguments, evidence, and overall effectiveness. This involves a deeper analysis, where you critically examine various aspects of the text to form a judgment about its quality and validity. This process sharpens your critical thinking abilities and promotes informed decision-making, equipping you to make sound choices in academic and everyday contexts. Evaluation is crucial because it transforms a passive activity into an engaging process, where you delve into underlying meanings, emotions and attitudes. It also develops your analytical skills, enabling you to analyze the structure, logic, and coherence of arguments, identifying strengths and weaknesses in the material. In academic settings, effective evaluation improves your academic performance, as excelling in this area often leads to better skills in writing persuasive essays, conducting research, and performing well in exams.

Tips to train and develop evaluation skill:

Even though a piece of writing is published, it is not necessarily accurate or free of bias. Therefore, you must look at published writings with a critical eye to gauge their trustworthiness. Generally, you can employ the following tips.

(1) Examine the source. Before getting down to the content, examine the publication information to determine its relevance and appropriateness. The author's bio can reveal their affiliation, such as a university, a newspaper, a website and past publication credits. The source indicates whether it is, a scholarly article, a news report, an interview, a story or a textbook chapter, and whether there are any potential biases. The date of publication helps you assess whether the information is still relevant and timely. The presence of a reference list shows the level and type of research the author conducted to gather evidence on the topic.

(2) Scrutinize the information. As you read, learn the information while simultaneously

questioning and scrutinizing it. Consider the following questions while reading:

——Has the author communicated clearly and organized the text well?

——Does the evidence support the argument and conclusions?

——Are there gaps in the logic?

——Has the author allowed their preference to influence the text?

——Has the author made generalizations or unreasonable assumptions?

(3) Utilize rubrics or checklists. To facilitate your evaluation, you can also turn to rubrics or checklists focusing on WHO, WHAT, WHEN, WHERE, HOW and WHY.

——Who is the author and what impact does this have on the quality of the information? Is the author trustworthy and qualified to provide that information? What is their academic specialization or experience in that subject area? Can you identify other work the author has published using other information sources? Who is the intended audience and how does this impact the information presented?

——What type of information is it and what does this mean for how you intend to use it? How well does this information relate to your search topic? Does it help answer your question, support or refute your arguments? Does it provide new information that you didn't know about until you read it? Is it useful because it provides a good definition and background knowledge, or is it too basic and you need something more in-depth and focused?

——When was the information published or made available online? Does the publication date impact the reliability of the information? Is this the most recent reference available on the topic? Are you looking for the latest findings within a subject or historical perspectives or trends? If it's from a website, does the site look maintained with few broken links? If it's from an eBook, is there a newer edition available? If it's a report or official source, are you given a version history or list of updates and amendments?

——Where? Which information source do you use to find the information and is that source appropriate for your need? Are you looking for academic sources? If so, was it published in a peer-reviewed journal? If you are looking for public opinion, professional literature, trade, or official publications, have you used sources that you recognize and trust?

——How did the author reach their conclusion? Are you able to follow the argument? How reliable and trustworthy are the results? Can you verify them? Is the author's idea supported by evidence or statistics? How does the information read? Does it sound objective?

——Why did the author write the information? Do you know how the writing was funded? Is it sponsored by a company, organization, or charity? Is the purpose to inform, teach, persuade, or sell?

Warm-up Questions

1. Do you know any famous diplomats from China?
2. Do you know any basic foreign policies of China?
3. What is the role of diplomacy in international relations?

Text

Outlook on China's Foreign Policy on Its Neighborhood in the New Era (Excerpt)

Significant Progress Made in China's Relations with Its Neighbors

Over the past half century and more, Asia, once plagued by poverty, weakness, turbulence and wars, has progressed successfully toward peace, stability, development, and prosperity. This is mainly accredited to the commitment of regional countries to independence, unity for strength, mutual respect, inclusiveness, mutual learning, mutual benefit and win-win cooperation. In this process, China and fellow Asian countries have jointly advocated the Five Principles of Peaceful Coexistence, carried forward the Bandung Spirit of solidarity, friendship and cooperation, and kept advancing good-neighborliness and mutually beneficial cooperation. Since the 18th National Congress of the CPC in 2012, China's relations with neighboring countries have been upgraded at a faster pace and produced fruitful results.

Political mutual trust has been growing. As of the date of this document's release, China has established diverse and substantive partnerships, cooperative relations and strategic relations of mutual benefit with 28 neighboring countries and ASEAN. China has reached common understandings with Pakistan, Laos, Cambodia, Myanmar, Indonesia, Kazakhstan, Tajikistan, Uzbekistan, Thailand, Mongolia, Turkmenistan, Malaysia and Kyrgyzstan on building a community with a shared future, and has agreed with the five Mekong countries to build a community with a shared future among Lancang-Mekong countries, and announced with the five Central Asian countries the decision to build a China-Central Asia community with a shared future. China has resolved historical boundary issues with 12 neighbors on land through negotiations and signed the treaties of good-neighborliness and friendly cooperation with nine neighboring countries. China has signed and ratified the Protocol to the Treaty on a Nuclear-Weapon-Free Zone in Central Asia, respects Mongolia's nuclear-weapon-free status, became the first to join the Treaty of Amity and Cooperation in Southeast Asia and is fully prepared to sign the Protocol to the Southeast Asia Nuclear-

Weapon-Free Zone Treaty at any time.

Mutual benefits keep deepening. China is the largest trading partner of 18 neighboring countries. In 2022, China's trade in goods with neighboring countries exceeded USD 2.17 trillion, up by 78 percent from 2012. The two-way investment between China and ASEAN has exceeded USD 380 billion in cumulative terms. China took the lead in ratifying the Regional Comprehensive Economic Partnership (RCEP) and worked for its entry into force and implementation, enabling and enhancing regional economic integration.

The Belt and Road Initiative (BRI) has delivered benefits to the neighborhood. China upholds the principle of planning together, building together and benefiting together, stays committed to the philosophy of open, green and clean cooperation, strives to achieve high-standard, sustainable and people-centered cooperation. China has signed BRI cooperation documents with 25 neighboring countries, and worked to synergize the BRI with cooperation plans of ASEAN and the Eurasian Economic Union. China has initiated the establishment of the Asian Infrastructure Investment Bank and the Silk Road Fund to provide financial support for infrastructure projects. Thanks to the joint efforts of all parties, a general connectivity framework consisting of six corridors, six connectivity routes and multiple countries and ports has been put in place. The fruitful BRI cooperation has spurred economic growth and improved people's lives in relevant countries and has injected strong impetus into economic recovery in the region.

Regional cooperation has grown in depth and substance. The Shanghai Cooperation Organization (SCO), co-founded by China and neighboring countries, has become a comprehensive regional organization with the largest geographical coverage and population. The China-Central Asia mechanism established by China and the five Central Asian countries has emerged as an important platform for in-depth cooperation between the six countries. Lancang-Mekong Cooperation is a success story of mutually beneficial cooperation in the sub-region, and the Lancang-Mekong Cooperation Economic Development Belt is taking shape. In a spirit of openness and inclusiveness, China actively participates in multilateral cooperation, including the ASEAN-centered East Asia cooperation mechanism, China-Japan-ROK cooperation, and Asia-Pacific Economic Cooperation (APEC), contributing to the region's integrated development and people's well-being.

Hotspot issues have been effectively managed and controlled. China has contributed solutions to political settlement of regional hotspot issues, and proposed and put into action the Chinese approach to addressing hotspot issues. On the Korean Peninsula issue, for the sake of peace, stability, and lasting security on the Peninsula, China has put forward the innovative "suspension-for-suspension" proposal and the dual-track approach, stayed committed to political settlement and actively facilitated peace talks. On Afghanistan, China has established a mechanism for coordination and cooperation among Afghanistan's neighbors, relaunched the China-Afghanistan-Pakistan Foreign Ministers' Dialogue, and issued the Tunxi Initiative on helping Afghanistan with reconstruction and development, building synergy among various parties. On Myanmar, China has encouraged the parties to bridge differences, restore social stability in the country, and launch political dialogue as quickly as possible.

Risks and challenges have been addressed effectively. China and neighboring countries have worked together in tackling such challenges as terrorism, separatism and financial crisis in the region. Since COVID-19 broke out, China and neighboring countries have come together to overcome difficulties, which reflects the spirit of a community with a shared future and leadership for global solidarity against the pandemic.

The remarkable progress made in Asia is attributable to the joint efforts of China and neighboring countries, and need to be cherished. China's development would not be possible without a peaceful and stable neighboring environment. The development of China and that of neighboring countries complement and reinforce each other. China's development will bring major opportunities and long-term benefits to countries across Asia, and will make even greater contributions to peace and development in the region.

A New Vision for the "Asian Century" in the New Era

In today's Asia, peace and stability reflect the overwhelming trend, and development and prosperity represent the aspiration of the people. China and regional countries share the same continent and the same ocean. Living and thriving here together, we share a common destiny and future. China will work with regional countries in solidarity to build a peaceful, secure, prosperous, beautiful, amicable and harmonious Asian home.

We need to jointly build a peaceful and secure home. The concept of peace, amity and harmony is Asian countries' remarkable contribution to human civilization. It is important to uphold peaceful coexistence, defend the red line of peace and stability, attach importance to the legitimate security concerns of all countries, and jointly respond to threats that undermine peace. China hopes to work with neighboring countries to cultivate long-term good-neighborliness and friendship, expand common ground while shelving and resolving differences, address differences and disputes between countries peacefully, and jointly safeguard enduring peace in the region. No matter what stage of development it reaches,

China will never seek hegemony or expansion. China will continue to work with ASEAN countries to fully and effectively implement the Declaration on the Conduct of Parties in the South China Sea (DOC) and actively advance consultations and conclusion of a Code of Conduct in the South China Sea (COC), and work with parties concerned in the South China Sea to properly address maritime disagreements and differences through dialogue. We need to strengthen maritime cooperation, deepen mutual trust and security, and promote joint development, in an effort to make the South China Sea a sea of peace, friendship and cooperation.

China will work with regional countries to manage regional security affairs with a coordinated approach. We need to enhance economic and financial security cooperation, deepen macro economic policy coordination, and bolster regional financial stability. It is important to advance cooperation in such fields as counterterrorism, deradicalization and fighting cross-border crimes, and enhance security cooperation on nuclear facilities, cyberspace, outer space and polar regions. We need to enhance the region's capacity in public health security governance, and strengthen cooperation in biosecurity, prevention and treatment of dangerous communicable diseases, medical supplies, and vaccine and pharmaceutical technologies. Cooperation on food and energy security needs to be enhanced to ensure the safety and stability of production and supply chains.

We need to jointly build a prosperous and beautiful home. China will continue to firmly pursue the strategy of openness, development and mutual benefit, raise the level of trade and investment facilitation and liberalization, deepen regional economic integration, and build a more open Asian big market. China will further expand trade with regional countries, increase imports from neighboring countries, and improve customs clearance facilitation. China will continue to promote the process of joining the Comprehensive and Progressive Agreement for Trans-Pacific Partnership (CPTPP) and the Digital Economy Partnership Agreement (DEPA). China stands ready to negotiate high-standard free trade agreements with more regional countries, improve the regional free trade network, and build a common big market. To promote high-quality BRI cooperation, China will give priority to connectivity corridor projects of railways and highways with neighboring countries, and accelerate the development of the New International Land-Sea Trade Corridor. We need to speed up development of the China-ASEAN Free Trade Agreement 3.0, effectively implement RCEP and work for its expansion and upgrading in due course. It is important to maintain the stable and smooth operation of industrial and supply chains to underpin open and inclusive cooperation. We need to vigorously develop the digital economy, strengthen exchange and cooperation in artificial intelligence, bio-medicine, modern energy and other fields, and translate scientific and technological innovation achievements into greater benefits to the people of regional countries.

China stands ready to work with regional countries to pursue green development and green growth model, drive economic growth with innovation, transform and upgrade economic, energy and industrial structures, and strike a fine balance between emission reduction and economic growth, in a bid to build an Asian home enjoying the concerted progress of economic growth and environmental progress. It is important to uphold the principle of common but differentiated responsibilities and strengthen climate cooperation. In the process of achieving carbon peaking and carbon neutrality, China stands ready to promote mutual learning and mutual benefit with neighboring countries, strengthen cooperation in green finance and green investment, and support low-carbon, sustainable development in the region. Efforts should be made to build a blue economic partnership and promote the sustainable development of the ocean.

We need to jointly build an amicable and harmonious home. We uphold mutual respect and equality in promoting exchanges, dialogue, inclusiveness and mutual learning among civilizations. It is important to extract nutrients from the millennia-long Asian civilization, to help forge the collective identity of the Asian value, way and tradition, expand people-to-people exchanges and cooperation in the region, and cement popular support for good-neighborliness. More measures need to be introduced to facilitate traveling. China will strengthen cooperation in vocational education, higher education and mutual recognition of educational certificates, provide more government scholarships and scholarships for various universities and majors for neighboring countries, and facilitate the traveling of international students. We will continue to promote exchanges in the fields of culture, arts, youth, tourism, localities, media, think tanks and non-governmental organizations, and strengthen cooperation on Asia's cultural and sports industry.

China stands ready to work with neighboring countries to, relying on the four pillars of connectivity, development, security and people-to-people exchanges and focusing on the six cooperation areas of the political sector, economy and trade, science and technology, security, people-to-people exchanges and global challenges, work for a community with a shared future among neighboring countries that features shared concepts, plans, benefits, security and responsibilities. We need to jointly build a demonstration area of high-quality BRI cooperation, and deepen "physical connectivity" of infrastructure and "institutional connectivity" of rules and standards. We will work together to build Global Development

Initiative pilot zone featuring more equitable, balanced and inclusive development partnership, Global Security Initiative pilot zone featuring an Asian pathway of security defined by planning together, building together and benefiting together, and Global Civilization Initiative pilot zone that boosts people-to-people exchanges and the mutual learning, harmonious coexistence of civilizations.

China will take an active part in East Asia cooperation, China-Central Asia mechanism, SCO, BRICS, APEC, Conference on Interaction and Confidence Building Measures in Asia (CICA) and other multilateral mechanisms and organizations, and strengthen dialogue and cooperation with the Pacific Islands Forum, Indian Ocean Rim Association and other regional organizations, in a bid to jointly promote the connectivity, stability and development of Asia, Pacific Ocean and Indian Ocean regions.

💡 Glossary

accredit v.	认为(……说法)出自
Five Principles of Peaceful Coexistence	和平共处五项原则
Bandung Spirit	万隆精神
ASEAN	东南亚国家联盟(Association of Southeast Asian Nations)
Southeast Asia Nuclear-Weapon-Free Zone Treaty	东南亚无核武器区条约
Regional Comprehensive Economic Partnership (RCEP)	区域全面经济伙伴关系协定
geographical coverage	地理覆盖范围
Lancang-Mekong Cooperation	澜沧江-湄公河合作
China-Japan-ROK cooperation	中日韩合作

Asia-Pacific Economic Cooperation (APEC)	亚太经济合作组织
Tunxi Initiative	屯溪倡议(国家在安徽省黄山市屯溪区提出的一项旨在促进文化遗产保护与可持续发展的倡议)
maritime *adj.*	海上的
Comprehensive and Progressive Agreement for Trans-Pacific Partnership (CPTPP)	全面与进步跨太平洋伙伴关系协定
Digital Economy Partnership Agreement (DEPA)	数字经济伙伴关系协定
amicable *adj.*	友好的
millennia-long	千年的
Global Development Initiative pilot zone	全球发展倡议试点区
Conference on Interaction and Confidence Building Measures in Asia (CICA)	亚洲相互协作与信任措施会议(亚信会议)

💡 Evaluation Reading Tasks

Task 1 Answer questions.

(1) Can you guess the source of this text? What can support your answer?

(2) How do you categorize this text? Is it a news report, a scholarly article, a textbook chapter, a speech to government officials or a different type? And how do you know that?

Task 2 Discuss.

This text argues that the remarkable progress made by Asia in terms of peace, stability, development, and prosperity over the past half-century is largely due to the commitment of regional countries, particularly China, to principles of mutual respect, inclusiveness, and cooperative development. Please figure out how the following aspects support the argument and whether they are sufficient, relevant, and reliable.

- political mutual trust
- mutual benefits and economic cooperation
- Belt and Road Initiative
- regional cooperation mechanisms
- management of hotspot issues
- addressing risks and challenges
- vision for the future

Text B

Major-Country Diplomacy Benefits the World-At-Large[①]

Poland is a major European agricultural producer, which exports large amounts of dairy products annually and China is one of its fastest growing markets. The China Railway Express (CRE) trains, which reduce transportation time from Poland to China—from 40 days by sea to around 14 days by land, are so crucial for Polish companies exporting agricultural goods to China. Agnieszka Maliszewska, director of the Polish Chamber of Milk, said the CRE has been "a very good choice" for them.

The CRE's development reflects on the amazing success story of the Belt and Road Initiative (BRI) and China's multilateral diplomacy. United Nations Secretary-General Antonio Guterres said, "China has become the most important pillar of multilateralism and an indispensable, trustworthy force for world peace and development."

Multilateralism can help to moderate over the impact of difficult issues and is therefore an important vehicle for a new type of international relations featured by win-win cooperation.

Since the 18th National Congress of the Communist Party of China (CPC), China has hosted a succession of diplomatic events in a bid to share China's voice, offering China's wisdom and proposing China's plan to the world through "host diplomacy". And Beijing has embraced the outside world with unprecedented openness through programs including the BRI.

In 2021, China's cross-border trade with countries among BRI member states has registered growth at 23.6 percent, 2.2 percentage points higher than the overall growth rate of China's foreign trade in the same period. Exports between China and BRI members have risen to an estimated 6.59 trillion yuan, up by 21.5 percent; while imports increased by 26.4 percent to 5.01 trillion yuan.

Since the BRI was put forward, China has promoted cooperation among nation states to meet the challenges, protect people's health and safety, facilitate the recovery of social

---

① This article was issued in 2022.

benefits and the economy, and unleash more growth potentials. So far, China has signed more than 200 documents on BRI cooperation with 149 countries and 32 international organizations. Building a community of shared future for humanity is the overall goal and the most distinctive feature of China's major-country diplomacy with Chinese characteristics in a new era.

Accordingly, efforts should be first focused on the periphery countries. After making initial progress in Africa—the continent that has the greatest number of developing countries, China has taken further steps to include developed countries by holding dialogues with political parties and building trust among the people.

At the state level, China is building bilateral communities of shared future with Laos, Cambodia, Myanmar, Pakistan, and many other countries across the globe. At the regional level, China enjoys more shared regional consensus with the Association of Southeast Asian Nations, Africa, Arab states, as well as Latin America on building the community. At the global level, China calls for building communities of a shared future in the areas of cyberspace, nuclear safety, maritime affairs and health.

Consequently, Beijing is achieving the great rejuvenation of the Chinese nation not to get ahead of the U.S. nor to bring back its ancient glory, but to build a community of shared future with the rest of the world. The concept is central to Xi Jinping Thought on Diplomacy, guiding major-country diplomacy with Chinese characteristics.

It is China's answer to such questions as "what happened to the world," "what should we do," "what kind of world should we build" and "how can we build such a world," in order to establish global connectivity through BRI cooperation.

Chinese President Xi Jinping, in his talks with foreign leaders, has repeatedly said, "the pandemic has once again proven that building a community of shared future is the only right path." Advancing the common values of humanity—peace, development, equity, justice, democracy and freedom, serve as a great banner for our times.

As humanity faces a growing governance deficit, trust deficit, development deficit, and peace deficit, the world today is witnessing changes on a scale unseen in a century's time. The international community looks to China for more and better global public goods.

Development is the solution for all problems and its pursuit is shared by people across the world. In his speech at the United Nations General Assembly on September 21, 2021, President Xi proposed a Global Development Initiative to enhance all people's well-being and realize all-round human development.

He called on the international community to give greater consideration to developing countries and to prioritize cooperation on poverty reduction, food security, COVID-19 response and vaccines, development financing, climate change, green development, industrialization, digital economy and connectivity. Therefore, greater global synergy can help to implement the *2030 Agenda for Sustainable Development*, which has received strong support from international organizations including the UN and nearly 100 countries.

Development should be sustainable and shared by all. By renewing commitments to the Sustainable Development Goals, revitalizing global partnerships, and reactivating international development cooperation, China has drawn up a roadmap for narrowing the North-South gap and addressing development imbalances in order to fulfill the *2030 Agenda for Sustainable Development*.

Besides, China has also built powerful synergy for more enhance robust, greener and more balanced development overall. The Global Development Initiative and BRI are constant sources for wisdom and inspiration in efforts to upgrade global governance for bringing about a better world.

Glossary

multilateralism *n.*	多边主义
indispensable *adj.*	不可或缺的
moderate *v.*	缓和
host diplomacy	主场外交
unprecedented *adj.*	前所未有的
register *v.*	(指数字等)被显示或记录
unleash *v.*	发挥,释放
deficit *n.*	赤字,不足
United Nations General Assembly	联合国大会
Global Development Initiative	全球发展倡议
synergy *n.*	协同作用
2030 Agenda for Sustainable Development	《2030年可持续发展议程》

Evaluation Reading Tasks

Task 1　Explain the following terms in your own words based on your research.

(1) Polish Chamber of Milk
(2) the Belt and Road Initiative
(3) a community of shared future for humanity
(4) Global Development Initiative
(5) global public goods
(6) the *2030 Agenda for Sustainable Development*

Task 2　Choose one of the topics and make a speech.

(1) China's involvement in key multilateral organizations

Examine China's involvement in organizations such as the United Nations, World Trade Organization, and BRICS (Brazil, Russia, India, China, South Africa). You can analyze China's contributions and roles within these organizations, as well as its efforts to promote cooperation, peace, and development at the global level. You can also assess the challenges and opportunities that China faces in its participation in multilateral diplomacy and the implications for its major-country status.

(2) Belt and Road Initiative (BRI) and major-country diplomacy

Do some research on the BRI, focusing on its impact on China's diplomacy. You can explore the BRI's economic and social implications, as well as its significance in China's major-country diplomacy. Evaluate the BRI's influence on China's relationships with other countries and its role in shaping the international order.

Text

China and Ireland Economic and Finance Cooperation①(Excerpt)

Before my arrival in China as Ambassador of Ireland, like anyone else embarking on a posting to the Middle Kingdom, I spent a lot of time becoming acquainted with the different aspects of the bilateral relations between Ireland and China.

While I expected to see a positive and robust relationship, I was still struck by the sheer variety of areas in which Ireland and China cooperate. Very high among these areas was of course our relationship as trading and economic partners.

Irish and Chinese economies have much in common—economies previously heavily reliant on agriculture, which have been transformed in a relatively short space of time into highly advanced and technologically innovative economies. Both our governments place a great emphasis on education and innovation as a means to raise living standards. We are both determined to add our own unique skills and competencies to the advancement of the global economy.

Ireland and China are also two of the few countries who recorded GDP growth in 2020 despite the challenges of COVID-19.

Bilateral Trade Flows

Aligned with our commonalities, we have witnessed continual growth in our trading relationship in the decades since the establishment of diplomatic relations in 1979. This growth has increased rapidly in the last number of years with bilateral trade in goods and services rising from approximately EUR 7 billion in 2013 to over EUR 24 billion in 2019.

Despite the current pandemic, we continue to enjoy very strong trade flows. The year

---

① This article was issued in 2022.

2020 witnessed approximately EUR 16.8 billion in trade in goods comprised of over EUR 10.5 billion in Irish exports to China and EUR 6.2 billion in imports from China to Ireland. This represents an impressive 18% year on year growth from 2019.

As well as an active flow of goods and services in both directions, Ireland also engages actively on the ground with China through its extensive physical Team Ireland presence. At present, Ireland is represented by our Embassy in Beijing, our resident Consulates General in Shanghai and Hong Kong and our State agencies across the cities of Beijing, Shanghai, Hong Kong and Shenzhen.

Enterprise Ireland, the IDA (Industrial Development Authority), Bord Bia and Tourism Ireland all play a major role in actively promoting Ireland in China and raising awareness of our country and its wide range of unique offerings across a multitude of sectors.

Enterprise Ireland is the government organization responsible for the development and growth of Irish enterprises in world markets by working in partnership with Irish companies to help them start, grow, innovate and win export sales in global markets.

IDA Ireland's main objective is to encourage investment into Ireland by foreign-owned companies. Bord Bia, Ireland's food promotion agency is responsible for bringing Ireland's outstanding food, drink and horticulture to the world, thus enabling growth and sustainability of producers. Tourism Ireland is responsible for marketing the island of Ireland overseas as a leading holiday destination.

In many cities across China, Ireland's Embassy, Consulate and State agency representatives work hard to promote Ireland and Irish businesses and companies introducing top-quality Irish produce to Chinese audiences. From trade and investment exhibitions, seafood and food and beverage trade fairs to education Expos and cultural promotion events, Team Ireland maximizes both physical and increasingly virtual events and opportunities to promote Ireland.

Ireland has enduring relationships with China's top international trade fairs, with participation in both the China International Import Exhibition (CIIE) in Shanghai and the China International Fair for Trade in Services (CIFTIS) in Beijing in recent years.

In terms of Chinese investment into Ireland, we continue to witness very strong growth in this area. Chinese foreign direct investment (FDI) into Ireland rose by 56% to EUR 130.5 million in 2019. 2020 saw further major Chinese investment into Ireland with Huawei expanding its Irish operations in terms of investment and employment and TikTok announcing in 2021 that it intended on establishing its first European data center in Ireland as part of a EUR 460 million investment into Ireland.

The Irish Government, with strong engagement from its Chinese counterpart, intends to capitalize on the extensive complementarities between, on the one hand, China's national economic priorities as set out in its 14th Five-Year Plan, and on the other hand, the strengths that Ireland has to offer. Ireland's particular strengths lie in innovation, entrepreneurship, science and technology including R&D, higher education, high technology including green, clean and fintech, financial services, food, agri-science and food safety systems.

Research and Development

Outside of trade flows, there are also many compatibilities between Chinese and Irish economies. Many of the highest priority areas contained in the recently announced 14th Five-Year Plan such as sustainable urbanization, innovation, research and development, green development and regional development are areas, in which key Irish policy makers have a keen interest. Furthermore, in many of these areas, Ireland is highly ranked in global rankings.

Ireland's global rankings in research and development have risen sharply in recent years with particularly strong performances in the following areas:

No. 1 ranking in Nanotechnology,

No. 2 ranking in Animal and Diary Science and Immunology,

No. 2 ranking in Computer Science,

No. 3 ranking in Animal Husbandry and Dairy Science, and

No. 5 ranking in Materials Science.

Irish higher education institutes are very much a part of the research and development ecosystem in Ireland and linked to this are their relationships with fellow educational institutes around the world. In terms of Ireland-China educational collaboration, there are now more than 200 joint higher education programs between educational institutes in China and Ireland.

Additionally, a revised memorandum of understanding to promote cooperation on science, technology and innovation was signed between Ireland and China in July 2019. This will allow our countries deepen our relationships in the area of research and innovation, which is also essential to deliver on our shared ambitions to become global innovation leaders.

Enduring people-to-people links between Ireland and China are very much in evidence in the education field in the thousands of students in Ireland and China, who seize the opportunity to study in our respective countries annually.

Financial Services

Expertise in internationally traded specialist financial services has been a core part of Ireland's offering to the world for over three decades. Ireland's proven capabilities across international banking, insurance, aviation financing, fintech and payments and asset management and fund services industries have been a constant source of growth and pride.

Connecting international asset managers from around the world with clients from 70 countries illustrates how Ireland's wider financial services sector operates as a gateway to Europe—we use our skills to build success for our partners and ourselves.

In April 2019, the Government of Ireland launched *Ireland for Finance*, its whole-of-government strategy for the further development of the international financial services sector in Ireland to 2025. The vision of the strategy for Ireland is to be a top-tier location of choice for specialist international financial services.

The employment target for the strategy is to reach 50,000 people in direct employment in the sector by 2025. This compares with 44,000 people directly employed in the sector at the end of 2018.

The strategy is structured around the following four pillars.

1. The operating environment pillar focuses on ensuring the policy, culture and legislative conditions underpinning international financial services will support growth.

2. The technology and innovation pillar focuses on providing a collaborative approach to addressing emerging challenges and opportunities in technological developments.

3. The talent pillar seeks to ensure that we continue to have skilled people to meet the demands of the international financial services sector, including meeting new and changing skills.

4. The communications and promotion pillar focus on ensuring that Ireland's international financial offering is communicated to all those who are or may be attracted to investing in Ireland.

Three horizontal priorities apply across the four pillars: regionalization, sustainable finance and diversity.

The Ireland for Finance Strategy also recognizes that organizations that are diverse improve collaboration and drive better financial performance by harnessing the power of different experiences, knowledge and skills. Within this space, gender diversity plays a crucial role and can enhance the process and quality of decision-making.

The key to building success in the long term is sustained investment in knowledge and relationships. Ireland can, and increasingly will, provide inbound access to investment managers looking to deploy capital in the Chinese securities markets—the previous work of industry participants around the Stock Connect infrastructure and grant of RQFII (RMB Qualified Foreign Institutional Investor) quota to Ireland in late 2016 are testament to this.

Just as important, the rapid development of asset management capabilities in China will naturally seek new markets and client bases to extend and increase the size of their international businesses. Ireland, as a global center for asset management and fund services, is ready to assist in this journey.

Glossary

bilateral trade	双边贸易
resident Consulates General	常驻总领事馆
IDA	工业发展局(Industrial Development Authority)
Bord Bia	爱尔兰食品局
beverage trade fair	饮料贸易展会
nanotechnology *n.*	纳米技术
immunology *n.*	免疫学
animal husbandry	畜牧业
dairy science	乳品科学
materials science	材料科学
memorandum *n.*	备忘录
fintech	金融科技
harness *v.*	利用,驾驭
RQFII	人民币境外合格机构投资者(RMB Qualified Foreign Institutional Investor),RQFII 境外机构投资者可将批准额度内的外汇结汇投资于境内的证券市场
quota *n.*	限额,配额,定额

Evaluation Reading Tasks

Task 1　Answer questions.

(1) Who is the author of the text? What does his identity inform you about the content of the text?

(2) How do you summarize the main idea or the author's main argument of the text?

(3) Does the author provide reliable and sufficient evidence for his argument?

(4) Has the author allowed his preference to influence the text?

(5) Has the author made generalizations or unreasonable assumptions?

Task 2　Discuss.

(1) Please find one more source on China-Ireland relations, and compare the information provided by the above text, discuss with your classmates how they are related and what your conclusion is on the bilateral ties.

(2) In the past decade, the bilateral trade relations between China and Ireland have witnessed a remarkable surge, marking a significant evolution in their economic ties. However, despite these economic advancements, cultural exchanges between China and Ireland have encountered challenges rooted in geographical and historical factors. Discuss with your classmates on the topic of "cultural exchanges between China and Ireland have been limited due to geographical and historical factors".

Practical Assignment

Make a speech.

Imagine yourself as the newly appointed Chinese Ambassador to Ireland, stepping into your role with a mission to strengthen bilateral ties between the two countries. On your first day in office, you are tasked with delivering a speech to mark the beginning of your ambassadorship. Based on the information of Text C, prepare a speech outlining your vision, priorities, and goals for strengthening the diplomatic relations between China and Ireland. Consider the historical ties, current challenges, and opportunities for collaboration in areas such as trade, culture, technology and education.

Digital Resource 3-1

Unit 4

Society

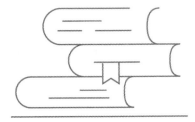

二十大报告选摘

Report to the 20th National Congress of the Communist Party of China (Excerpt)

我们深入贯彻以人民为中心的发展思想,在幼有所育、学有所教、劳有所得、病有所医、老有所养、住有所居、弱有所扶上持续用力,人民生活全方位改善。

We have implemented a people-centered philosophy of development. We have worked continuously to ensure people's access to childcare, education, employment, medical services, elderly care, housing, and social assistance, thus bringing about an all-around improvement in people's lives.

坚持农业农村优先发展,坚持城乡融合发展,畅通城乡要素流动。加快建设农业强国,扎实推动乡村产业、人才、文化、生态、组织振兴。

We will continue to put agricultural and rural development first, pursue integrated development of urban and rural areas, and facilitate the flows of production factors between them. We will move faster to build up China's strength in agriculture and steadily promote the revitalization of businesses, talent, culture, ecosystems, and organizations in the countryside.

我们要坚持教育优先发展、科技自立自强、人才引领驱动,加快建设教育强国、科技强国、人才强国,坚持为党育人、为国育才,全面提高人才自主培养质量,着力造就拔尖创新人才,聚天下英才而用之。

We will continue to give high priority to the development of education, build China's self-reliance and strength in science and technology, and rely on talent to pioneer and to propel development. We will speed up work to build a strong educational system, greater scientific and technological strength, and a quality workforce. We will continue efforts to cultivate talent for the Party and the country and comprehensively improve our ability to nurture talent at home. All this will see us producing first-class innovators and attracting the brightest minds from all over.

深化医药卫生体制改革,促进医保、医疗、医药协同发展和治理。促进优质医疗资源扩容和区域均衡布局,坚持预防为主,加强重大慢性病健康管理,提高基层防病治病和健康管理能力。深化以公益性为导向的公立医院改革,规范民营医院发展。发展壮大医疗卫生队伍,把工作重点放在农村和社区。重视心理健康和精神卫生。促进中医药传承创新发展。创新医防协同、医防融合机制,健全公共卫生体系,提高重大疫情早发现能力,加强重大疫情防控救治体系和应急能力建设,有效遏制重大传染性疾病传播。深入开展健康中国行动和爱国卫生运动,倡导文明健康生活方式。

We will further reform the medical and healthcare systems and promote coordinated development and regulation of medical insurance, medical services, and pharmaceuticals. We will expand the availability of quality medical resources and ensure they are better distributed among regions. Giving priority to prevention, we will strengthen health management for major chronic diseases and enhance the capacity for disease prevention and treatment as well as health management at the community level. We will deepen reform of public hospitals to see that they truly serve the public interest and better regulate the development of private hospitals. We will build up the ranks of medical and healthcare personnel with an emphasis on rural areas and urban communities. We will place importance on mental and psychological health. We will promote the preservation and innovative development of traditional Chinese medicine. We will develop new mechanisms for enhancing collaboration and integration between hospitals and institutions for disease prevention and control. We will also improve the public health system, improve our early warning system for major epidemics, and strengthen the systems for epidemic prevention, control, and treatment as well as our emergency response capacity so as to effectively contain major infectious diseases. We will further advance the Healthy China Initiative and patriotic health campaigns and promote sound, healthy lifestyles.

Critical Reading Skill—Interpretation

Why is interpretation important for critical reading?

Interpretation is the process of deriving meaning from a text by analyzing its components and considering various perspectives. It involves going beyond the surface-level understanding of the words to uncover deeper significance, attitudes and implications. Interpretation requires you to examine the context, author's intent, language, and structure of the text. It also involves considering your own experiences to understand how they might influence your reading. By interpreting a text, you engage in a dialogue with it, questioning and reflecting on its messages, which ultimately leads to a more nuanced and informed understanding.

Through interpretation, you can analyze how different elements of a text—such as language, structure, and context—contribute to its overall meaning. This process helps you engage more thoughtfully with the material, considering multiple perspectives and drawing informed conclusions. Additionally, interpretation enables you to connect the text to broader themes, societal issues, and personal experiences, enriching your comprehension and making the reading experience more relevant.

Tips to train and develop interpretation skill:

Interpretation is a cornerstone of critical reading. In order to train and develop the skill, you can try the following tips.

(1) Preview. Preview the title, subtitles, headings, and any visual aids like charts, graphs, or illustrations before diving into the text. This can provide a sense of the main topic and structure of the text.

(2) Consider the context. Understand the context in which the text was written. Consider the historical, cultural, and social context that may influence the author's perspective and the message conveyed in the text.

(3) Analyze. Closely examine the language, structure, and stylistic features of the text. Analyze the author's use of vocabulary, imagery, and figurative language to understand the author's purpose, tone, point of view and implicit information of the text.

(4) Research further. If you encounter unfamiliar concepts or ideas, take the initiative to research further to gain a deeper understanding. Explore related topics and different sources to clarify, reflect and broaden your knowledge.

Warm-up Questions

1. What has China done to reduce poverty?
2. How do you describe the development in China's education?
3. Are there any examples to show that remarkable changes have taken place in China's healthcare?

Text

Poverty Alleviation: China's Experience and Contribution (Excerpt)

Exploring a new path of poverty alleviation

Eliminating poverty is a challenge for all countries. Each subject to different national conditions and at different stages of development, they adopt different poverty reduction criteria, methods and approaches. Bearing in mind its prevailing reality and understanding the nature of poverty and the status of poverty alleviation, China has embarked on a path of poverty alleviation and designed an approach with Chinese characteristics. In this battle, the nation has upheld the CPC leadership and the people-centered philosophy. It has taken advantage of one of the strengths of its socialist system—the ability to pool resources on major endeavors. It has adopted targeted measures and stimulated the enthusiasm, initiative, and creativity of the people in poverty. It has carried forward the great tradition of working together and offering mutual support, and it has adopted a down-to-earth and pragmatic style of work. In this approach, China has accumulated valuable experience, which belongs both to China itself and to the rest of the world, and offers enlightenment to the international community in its battle to reduce poverty.

1. People-centered philosophy

The CPC is a party with a grand but simple goal: to ensure a happy life for the Chinese people. In the face of all the changes in the international landscape and the domestic situation over the past century, the Party has always followed a people-centered philosophy. It has borne in mind its founding mission to seek happiness for the Chinese people and national rejuvenation, and united and led the people in fighting poverty armed with firm convictions and a strong will. In the new era, the CPC has adopted a series of bold policies and measures to advance the cause, trying to ensure higher incomes and better education, healthcare, and living conditions for the poor. Taking public satisfaction as an important yardstick to judge the effectiveness of poverty elimination, the Party has concentrated its efforts on guaranteeing the basic needs of the poor. It would rather cut down on the number of major projects in favor of investment in poverty elimination; it would rather penalize short-term, partial or local interests to ensure the cause is well served and guaranteed; and it would rather slow the pace of economic growth to ensure the task of poverty alleviation is accomplished on schedule.

...

China's poverty elimination effort in the new era is a full and vivid expression of its people-centered philosophy and the CPC's mission of serving the people wholeheartedly. Success in poverty alleviation has proven that the problem of poverty, in essence, is how the people should be treated: The people-centered philosophy is the fundamental driving force behind this cause. Only with this philosophy, can a country identify those who are poor, adopt concrete measures, and deliver genuine outcomes; only with this philosophy, can it draw on inexhaustible motivation, set a clear direction, and find the right approach.

2. Highlighting poverty alleviation in the governance of China

...

The CPC has always regarded poverty alleviation as an important task for ensuring national peace and stability. It has highlighted poverty alleviation at national level when setting its guidelines, principles and policies, and when formulating national plans for medium- and long-term development. The Party has pooled national resources to advance this cause and motivated generations of its members to devote themselves to this cause.

...

The success in poverty alleviation has proven that governance of a country starts with the needs of the people, and that their prosperity is the responsibility of the government. Poverty alleviation is a pioneering and arduous trek. To achieve success, it is of utmost importance that the leadership has devotion, strong will and determination, and the ruling party and government assume their responsibilities to the people, play a leading role, mobilize forces from all quarters, and ensure policies are consistent and stable.

3. Eradicating poverty through development

The root cause of poverty is inadequate development. As the world's largest developing country with a population of over 1.4 billion, China is aware that development is essential to solving many of its problems, including poverty. The CPC has always regarded this as the top priority in governing and rejuvenating the country. It has concentrated its efforts in particular on the economy, to address the problem of unbalanced and inadequate development. Through development, the economy has been growing rapidly and the country has enjoyed a long period of social stability. China has regarded reform as an important driving force for poverty eradication and worked constantly to remove institutional and structural causes of poverty:

- By launching land reform and establishing the socialist system after the founding of the PRC in 1949;
- By implementing the household contract responsibility system with remuneration linked to output after the launch of reform and opening up in 1978;
- By establishing the socialist market economy and rescinding all agricultural taxes;
- By separating the ownership rights, contracting rights, and management rights for contracted rural land and further reforming the rural collective property rights system since the 18th CPC National Congress in 2012.

These measures have contributed to rural development and increased farmers' incomes. In addition, China has opened wider to the world amidst economic globalization and seen sustained and rapid growth in its foreign trade, creating many employment opportunities and more sources of higher incomes for rural labor.

...

China's experience with poverty alleviation has proven that development is the most effective way to eradicate poverty and the most reliable path towards a more prosperous life. Only development can lead to economic growth, social progress and higher living standards. Only development can better guarantee people's basic rights and meet their desire for a better life.

4. Pressing ahead with poverty alleviation based on reality

Poverty problems, as well as their causes, are diverse and complex. China's poverty alleviation efforts are based on a realistic appraisal of the situation. China has set its poverty line and its poverty alleviation goals and strategies, and worked to create better ideas and methods based on its national conditions and stage of development, and on the changes in the demographics, distribution, and structure of the poor population. It has advanced this undertaking step by step and with a steady effort.

...

5. Letting the poor play the principal role

Poor people are the main players in eliminating poverty. Poverty alleviation requires both external and internal forces to form a synergy. China fully respects the principal role of the poor and encourages them to play their part, inspires them with the motivation to fight poverty, and enhances their ability to participate in development, share the fruits of development, and achieve endogenous development. They benefit from success in the undertaking of poverty alleviation and at the same time contribute to development in China.

China has inspired its people in poverty to strive for prosperity and provided them necessary education, so that they have the ambition to emerge from poverty and the tools to succeed. People in poverty have had better access to education opportunities, such as farmers' night schools and training workshops, to improve their skills and abilities in work and business.

A significant improvement in the battle against poverty is an effective mechanism of positive incentives encouraging the poor to learn from and keep pace with each other. Through this mechanism, productive activities are rewarded and subsidized and jobs instead of grants are provided, to encourage poor people to rely on their own efforts rather than wait for external assistance.

China has promoted stories of role models who escaped poverty through their hard work. It has also carried out various activities to establish the idea that "it is better to work hard than to endure poverty". The people in poverty have followed suit and eventually shaken off poverty and backwardness.

The fight against poverty shows that the people are the creators and drivers of history, and the true heroes. As long as a country serves the people, relies on them, respects their principal status and pioneering spirit, and motivates the poor to rely on their own hard work, it is sure to defeat poverty.

6. Pooling all resources to create synergy

Poverty alleviation is an arduous, complex, and systematic endeavor, requiring the active participation of all parties. In the fight against poverty, the CPC has mobilized and pooled all possible forces on the basis of its rigorous organizational system and efficient work mechanism. A large-scale poverty alleviation network has been established, with the government, society and the market working in coordination, and government-sponsored projects, sector-specific programs, and corporate and societal assistance supplementing each other. It is a framework with the full participation of multiple players from different regions, sectors, departments and businesses.

...

China has designated a National Poverty Alleviation Day and established a national system to commend models in fighting poverty. All these measures have created an atmosphere where everyone who is interested can join in poverty alleviation. China's experience has proven that only when a country mobilizes all sectors of society to unite with common purpose and act in unison, can poverty be finally defeated.

Under the CPC leadership, the Chinese people have created an approach to poverty alleviation with their own hard work. China's successful practice and valuable experience in eliminating extreme poverty have deepened human understanding of poverty alleviation trends, enriched and extended the theory of international poverty alleviation, and boosted the confidence of other countries, especially developing ones, in eradicating extreme poverty. They serve as reference for other countries to choose a suitable path of poverty alleviation, and offer China's approach to solving the problem of modern national governance and creating brighter prospects for social progress.

Glossary

pragmatic *adj.*	务实的
penalize *v.*	处罚
inexhaustible *adj.*	取之不尽的
eradicate *v.*	根除
household contract responsibility system	家庭联产承包责任制
remuneration *n.*	报酬
appraisal *n.*	评估
incentive *n.*	激励

Interpretation Reading Tasks

Task 1　Answer questions.

(1) What is the focus of this text, and how does the author establish its context?

(2) What is the tone of the author? Could you identify any specific words, phrases, or expressions to support your interpretation?

Task 2　Discuss.

Pay special attention to the cultural elements in this text. How do cultural values, such as emphasis on collective efforts and the role of individuals within the community contribute to China's strategy and experience in poverty alleviation? Discuss with your classmates and exchange your answers in class.

Text B

MOE Press Conference Presents China's Educational Achievements in 2023 (Excerpt)

Following the release of information, journalists inquired about the statistics. Here are the highlights from the Q&A session.

CCTV correspondent:

You just mentioned that the gross enrollment rate of higher education exceeded 60% in 2023, marking an improvement over 2022. As enrollment continues to expand, what are the next steps for optimizing the structure of higher education, in order to produce high-caliber future workers?

Guo Peng, Director-General of the Department of Development Planning, MOE:

Thank you for your question. As President Xi Jinping instructed at a recent meeting, our education system must focus on enhancing the overall quality of human resources to support China's modernization efforts. The MOE, in collaboration with the National Development and Reform Commission and the Ministry of Finance, is committed to aligning educational initiatives with the evolving needs of economic and social development. Our shared goal is to be responsive to the aspirations of the general public by expanding access to high-quality higher education resources and extending the duration of education for all. The recent achievement of a gross enrollment rate in higher education exceeding 60% is a significant step forward in developing high-quality human resources.

I want to underscore the significance of examining the depth and structure of talent development, while expanding the scale of higher education, particularly for nurturing high-caliber future workforce. Our focus is on several critical areas.

Firstly, we are committed to continuously expanding the scope of graduate-level education. Based on our vision of establishing a strong education system by 2035 and recognizing the link between education, science, and human resource development, we make graduate education policies by taking into account economic and social trends, national strategic imperatives, demographic shifts, and the natural dynamics of higher education. In recent years, the number of graduate students, particularly doctoral candidates, has steadily increased, laying the groundwork for high-quality economic development.

Secondly, we are constantly improving the structure of education to better prepare the best minds for future jobs. We are committed to developing both academic and innovation-focused talent by enhancing the enrollment opportunities for graduate students pursuing vocational degrees in applied fields, such as engineering and technology. In 2023, nearly 60% of students enrolled in vocational degree programs. In response to the changing technology landscape, we are assisting universities in enhancing their disciplinary structures, increasing their investment in developing STEM talent, and accelerating the training of innovators in science and technology. In 2023, the enrollment in master's programs in science, engineering, agriculture, and medicine reached 60%, while doctoral enrollment exceeded 80%.

Thirdly, we are continuously expanding our talent pool in key science and technology sectors. We are committed to creating high-quality talent centers and innovation hubs, as well as expanding graduate education in core disciplines and strategically important areas. We are also improving the link between science and education, fostering collaborations between leading academic institutions and research organizations, and promoting innovation in important scientific projects to enhance the technological independence of our nation.

Moving forward, we will put more energy into cultivating top talent by enhancing the scope, organization, and caliber of higher education. The goal is to provide essential and strategic support for China's modernization drive.

Southern Metropolis Daily correspondent:

According to the press conference, the total number of students enrolled in higher education nationwide has reached 47,631,900. With this sheer scale of enrollment in higher education, ensuring the quality of education and producing high-caliber graduates must be a challenge. In recent years, the MOE has made efforts to promote new and interdisciplinary areas of study, such as engineering, medical science, agricultural science and liberal arts. What is the latest progress in these fields?

Gao Dongfeng, Deputy Director-General of the Department of Higher Education, MOE:

Thank you for your question and for your interest in and support for China's higher education.

In recent years, the higher education sector has actively served the needs of our nation's strategic goals, by initiating proactive reforms in line with the important directives on higher education from President Xi, as well as decisions by the Party Central Committee and the State Council. Our focus remains on building new productive forces, by introducing new majors and promoting cross-disciplinary integration. We've systematically advanced the introduction of new engineering, medical, agricultural, and liberal arts disciplines. We're transforming strategies into goals and implementing goals into measures. We have achieved a series of breakthroughs in the organizational models, training mechanisms, content generation and teaching methods. These efforts represent a comprehensive effort to modernize and enhance the quality of higher education well suited to China's unique cultural, social, and economic context.

Firstly, we are driving significant reforms in our education system to better prepare our workforce for the future. Our emphasis on strategic emerging fields like AI, semiconductors, quantum science, healthcare, and energy has led to the establishment of specialized colleges and programs, including 12 future-proof tech institutes, 50 modern industry-focused colleges, 33 centers of excellence in software engineering, 28 microelectronics colleges, and 18 high-level public health colleges. These initiatives are transforming the way we teach and learn, allowing us to provide targeted, high-quality education.

Secondly, we are breaking down the barriers between academic disciplines, industry, and research to create a more dynamic and innovative education ecosystem. By collaborating with key stakeholders, we have set up 45 national innovation hubs that bring together the best minds from academia and industry to tackle pressing challenges in fields like chip design, clean energy, biotech, medical research, and AI. These hubs have already taken on over 1,100 projects of national significance, driving cutting-edge research and development. Moreover, we are doubling down on our efforts to foster deep partnerships between universities and businesses. By focusing on critical areas like sustainability, digital transformation, and quantum computing, we are creating powerful clusters of expertise and innovation.

Thirdly, we are focusing on cultivating top-notch innovative talent in fundamental disciplines. Across 77 of our leading universities, we have established nearly 300 specialized programs dedicated to cultivating the brightest minds in these critical disciplines. We have launched an ambitious International Summer School Program. This initiative has already seen 46 of our top universities host 112 summer schools, bringing together over 1,300 leading scholars from around the world to teach more than 1,100 courses. These summer schools have provided unparalleled opportunities for over 31,000 students to engage in cross-cultural exchanges and intellectual discourse. In addition, we are undertaking a comprehensive effort to strengthen the core components of our basic disciplines through the "101 Plan". This initiative spans nine key fields, from computer science and mathematics to medicine and economics. We have developed a curriculum structure of 12 core courses, authored 21 state-of-the-art textbooks, and established a practice platform encompassing over 400 projects.

Lastly, we are increasing our investments in fostering students' innovation. Just last year, we hosted a major international innovation competition that drew an astonishing level of participation—4.21 million projects and 17.09 million students from 5,296 schools across 151 countries and territories. We're also implementing a national-level program for college student innovation training, with 41,956 projects approved in 2023 involving 178,090 students and over 50,000 faculty members.

As we look to the future, our mission is clear—to build a world-class education system that powers the growth and prosperity of our nation. Our strategy is threefold. First, we will create a seamless loop of education, research, and talent development, ensuring that our universities are at the cutting edge of scientific and technological advancement. Second, we will focus on tackling the most pressing challenges facing our society, from plugging skills gaps to pioneering new fields of study. And third, we will double down on our efforts to cultivate top-tier talent across the disciplines of engineering, medicine, agriculture, and the liberal arts. We also recognize the transformative potential of emerging technologies like AI. That's why we're building a new ecosystem that combines the best of AI and education, creating powerful tools for personalized learning, adaptive assessment, and intelligent tutoring. Our goal is to provide talent support for overcoming bottlenecks and leading China's modernization efforts.

Glossary

high-caliber *adj.*	高素质的
MOE	教育部（Ministry of Education）
National Development and Reform Commission	国家发展和改革委员会
underscore *v.*	强调

imperative *n.*	必须要做的事，重要紧急的事
demographic shift	人口变化
dynamic *n.*	变化，动态
STEM	科学、技术、工程和数学（Science, Technology, Engineering, and Mathematics）
interdisciplinary *adj.*	跨学科的
Deputy Director-General	副司长
proactive *adj.*	积极主动的
Party Central Committee and the State Council	党中央和国务院
semiconductor *n.*	半导体
quantum science	量子科学
microelectronics *n.*	微电子学
top-notch *adj.*	顶尖的
seamless loop	无缝循环

 Interpretation Reading Tasks

Task 1 Answer questions.

(1) How do the tones of both correspondents reflect their concerns or interests regarding China's higher education?

(2) Do you think Mr. Guo Peng and Mr. Gao Dongfeng answered the correspondents' questions, and are their answers clear, concise and relevant?

(3) If you have the opportunity to ask one question on behalf of the Chinese college students, what question will you ask concerning China's higher education, and who would you like to answer your question, why?

(4) What cultural values are reflected in the emphasis on producing high-caliber graduates through higher education in China?

(5) Why does the Ministry of Education prioritize expanding graduate-level education, especially in STEM fields? How do you interpret their emphasis?

Task 2　Explain the following terms based on your research.

(1) National Development and Reform Commission
(2) 101 Plan
(3) new engineering, medical, agricultural, and liberal arts disciplines
(4) International Summer School Program

Text

8 Reasons Why China is the Most Exciting Healthcare Story in the World Right Now[①]

I have had the privilege of living in China for well over a decade. The healthcare market has changed dramatically during this time, and it has never been a dull experience to follow its development. I have come to the conclusion, though, that the China market has never been more exciting than it is today. Here are 8 reasons why.

1. The potential for patient and economic impact is gigantic

Healthy China 2030, China's national healthcare strategy published in 2016, has set ambitious targets for improving health outcomes for the Chinese population. Progress has already been made. For example, life expectancy of Chinese women and men has improved from 68 to 77 in the last 30 years.

But so much more can be done, especially in the context of a rapidly aging society. By 2030, the hope of the Chinese government is to create a 16 trillion RMB broader healthcare ecosystem by continuously strengthening preventative care, optimizing healthcare management and services, and taking care of key segments of the population, such as women and children. Taken together, these initiatives could translate into billions of additional life years, and will have an enormous impact on productivity and economic development in China.

---

① The author of this text is Franck Le Deu. He is a Senior Partner in the Hong Kong Office of McKinsey & Company, where he leads the Greater China Healthcare practice and is also co-leader of the Asia Pharma and MedTech practice.

2. Chinese labs are starting to crank out innovation

The signs are all here: A wave of "sea turtles" returning to China to seek their fortunes, abundant sources of funding, direct support by central and local government, unprecedented speed of decision-making and execution by regulators, and a degree of freedom to operate not always seen even in the West.

These are all feeding a rapidly expanding petri dish of innovation that is starting to yield tangible scientific outcomes. New molecules for colorectal cancer (fruquintinib discovered by Chi-Med), CAR-T, PD-1, are just a few concrete examples. Beyond these cases, there's the emergence of innovative MedTech companies (e.g., Venus MedTech in minimally invasive heart valves), next generation sequencing companies (e.g., Berry Genomics), or big data companies (e.g. LinkDoc, focused on oncology and already valued at $1 Billion, four years after it was started). Just a few years ago, developments such as these would have been unthinkable.

3. Fast and furious reform at the CFDA/NMPA

It's fair to say that the reform initiated in late 2015 by the CFDA (China Food and Drug Administration), now under NMPA (National Medical Products Administration), has been broader, deeper, and has moved faster than anyone could have anticipated. My McKinsey colleagues across sectors, would agree that this is largely unmatched by other sectors in China. The degree to which innovations that originate in China are being integrated into global drug trials and launches is unprecedented, and the success rate is tangible, with around 100 new drugs approved since 2016, setting a new record.

Achievements also include the publication of a rare disease list, creation of a fast track mechanism, acceptance of foreign data for registration, and the definition of a conditional approval pathway. "Any news from the CFDA is bad news" has now become, "any news from the NMPA is positive". Some multinationals have seen their new drug candidates attain such swift approval they've had to scramble to get them to market.

4. Renewed optimism at pharma MNCs

It may be cyclical, but we are clearly experiencing another period of "peak optimism" among MNCs (Multinational Corporations), fueled by very strong commercial performance of their affiliates (many are growing at 15~20% this year and exceeding budget), "fast and furious" CFDA reform, and the realization that the Chinese market is at an inflection point when it comes to opportunities for partnership and innovation.

Some multinationals are becoming more China-centric in their global strategy, even placing a number of key global management positions in China. The contribution of China revenues to global businesses continues to rise, and now stands at over 10% for a handful of companies. Of course, companies are fully cognizant of the uncertainties they face. For example, increasing pressure on mature brands, particularly with the impending roll-out of the Generics Quality Consistency Evaluation initiative, and access bottlenecks that still constrain the uptake of new drugs.

5. The PAT are here to disrupt healthcare

The so-called "BAT" triumvirate of Internet giants—Baidu, Alibaba, and Tencent—has recently morphed into "PAT"-PingAn, Alibaba, and Tencent. It's a reflection of the rapid emergence of three high tech giants that are making a large bet on healthcare. In just a few years, they have developed complex ecosystems allowing them to impact the full patient care value chain. More recent entrants such as JD.com, which has deep logistics expertise and reach, are also well positioned to disrupt traditional models. Perhaps we'll see more changes to that three-letter acronym in the future.

6. China cash is available and actively looking for opportunities, globally

We estimated that in 2017 more than $40 billion of cash was raised by healthcare focused funds, with over $10 billion deployed in funding deals. The trend has slowed down in 2018, but Chinese funds are playing an increasingly visible role supporting US based biotech (e.g., Grail, Viela Bio, IDEAYA), and are also starting to turn their eyes towards Europe, where many biotechs could benefit from access to new sources of cash. Leading Chinese funds such as Qiming Venture Partners, C-Bridge, 6 Dimensions Capital, 8 Roads Ventures, or Ally Bridge are building an ecosystem of innovation that has increasing global reach.

7. Make way for the HKEX train

In just one year, we have moved from expressions of intent to open up the HKEX to high tech companies, to the reality of having four companies already listed—Ascletis, BeiGene, Hua Medicine, and Innovent Bio—and with many more waiting to list, such as CStone, MicuRx, Frontage Laboratories, AOBiome Therapeutics, and Stealth Bio Therapeutics. The development of a true biotech cluster in Hong Kong will take time, however. Many elements of the ecosystem are still in an embryonic phase, and the pitfalls companies face are numerous, as evidenced by the poor stock performance of several early listers. But recent developments are providing a healthy dose of encouragement Chinese entrepreneurs dreaming of creating their own healthcare-focused game changer.

8. Chinese biotechs come of age?

Beyond the HKEX trend, we are seeing the initial wave of Chinese biotechs getting close to reaching the market with new drugs. Sure, most fall into the "me too" category, but a few are truly innovative, proving that homegrown innovation in China is possible. The emergence of these innovative players is also serving as a wake-up call for MNCs, who have to respond by adapting their talent value proposition, as well as their operating model. In just a few months, we have seen leaders of companies such as Pfizer, AstraZeneca, Roche, and J&J, move from senior positions at their companies to pre-eminent roles at biotechs. This first wave is one thing. The next wave will be another one altogether.

I probably could have highlighted a few more exciting trends, such as the change in provider landscape and improvements in private healthcare insurance. But these eight reasons should prove why China is such an exciting place to witness the development of the healthcare industry.

Glossary

petri dish *n.*	培养皿
colorectal cancer	结直肠癌
CAR-T	嵌合抗原受体 T 细胞免疫疗法（Chimeric Antigen Receptor T-Cell Immunotherapy），是一种治疗肿瘤的新型精准靶向疗法
PD-1	程序性死亡蛋白 1（Programmed Death-1），是一种重要的免疫抑制分子
sequencing company	测序公司
oncology *n.*	肿瘤学
CFDA	国家食品药品监督管理总局（China Food and Drug Administration）

NMPA	国家药品监督管理局(National Medical Products Administration)
MNC	跨国公司(Multinational Corporation)
inflection point	拐点,转折点
revenue *n*.	收入,收益
cognizant *adj*.	认识,认知的
impending *adj*.	即将发生的,迫近的
roll-out *n*.	新产品的推出
Generics Quality Consistency Evaluation	仿制药质量和疗效一致性评价
triumvirate *n*.	三巨头,三人团
morphed into	变成
entrant	新成员,进入者
HKEX	香港交易所,港交所,香港交易及结算所有限公司(Hong Kong Exchanges and Clearing Limited)
embryonic *adj*.	萌芽期的,刚起步的
pitfall *n*.	陷阱,困难,错误
entrepreneur *n*.	企业家
coming of age	成年

 Interpretation Reading Tasks

Task 1　Decide whether the following statements are TRUE or FALSE.

(1)(　　) The target readers of the text are probably Chinese families, especially the elders.

(2)(　　) In the context of a rapidly aging society, China's development of the healthcare industry will encounter unprecedented difficulties.

(3) (　) The fifth subheading—"The PAT are here to disrupt healthcare" does not support the author's argument.

(4) (　) Without the returning of "sea turtles" to China, the Chinese lab can hardly yield innovation.

(5) (　) Despite the previous pitfalls, the Chinese entrepreneurs dreaming of creating their own healthcare-focused game changer are bound to succeed.

(6) (　) Innovation is crucial for the development of Chinese biotechs.

Task 2　Answer the questions.

(1) What is the purpose or intention of the author, and what is your supporting evidence?

(2) What is the context of Text C, and does the context influence the author's perspective?

(3) What is the tone and attitude of the author? Is it objective and formal? Is it optimistic and hopeful? Is it watchful? Is it aloof? How do you know that?

(4) What does the author mean by saying "This first wave is one thing. The next wave will be another one altogether." in the end?

Practical Assignment

Conduct an interview.

1. Please interview 1 or 2 teachers who have taught for about 30 years in your university or a high school or primary school. Ask the teacher/teachers to talk about the changes they have witnessed in Chinese education over the past 20~30 years. Prepare questions or a guideline focusing on some aspects of education, and take notes or record the interview. After analyzing the interview data, present your findings in class.

2. Please interview your grandparents or some senior citizens around you. Ask them to talk about how China's healthcare in the past differs from the healthcare of today, and in what aspects it has significantly improved and what are their expectations in this regard. Take notes or record the interview. After analyzing the interview data, share your findings in class.

Digital Resource 4-1

Unit 5

Environment

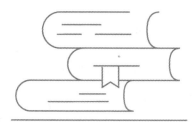

二十大报告选摘

Report to the 20th National Congress of the Communist Party of China (Excerpt)

我们坚持绿水青山就是金山银山的理念,坚持山水林田湖草沙一体化保护和系统治理,全方位、全地域、全过程加强生态环境保护,生态文明制度体系更加健全,污染防治攻坚向纵深推进,绿色、循环、低碳发展迈出坚实步伐,生态环境保护发生历史性、转折性、全局性变化,我们的祖国天更蓝、山更绿、水更清。

We have acted on the idea that lucid waters and lush mountains are invaluable assets. We have persisted with a holistic and systematic approach to conserving and improving mountain, water, forest, farmland, grassland, and desert ecosystems, and we have ensured stronger ecological conservation and environmental protection across the board, in all regions, and at all times. China's ecological conservation systems have been improved, the critical battle against pollution has been advanced, and solid progress has been made in promoting green, circular, and low-carbon development. This has led to historic, transformative, and comprehensive changes in ecological and environmental protection and has brought us bluer skies, greener mountains, and cleaner waters.

中国式现代化是人与自然和谐共生的现代化。人与自然是生命共同体,无止境地向自然索取甚至破坏自然必然会遭到大自然的报复。我们坚持可持续发展,坚持节约优先、保护优先、自然恢复为主的方针,像保护眼睛一样保护自然和生态环境,坚定不移走生产发展、生活富裕、生态良好的文明发展道路,实现中华民族永续发展。

It is the modernization of harmony between humanity and nature. Humanity and nature make up a community of life. If we extract from nature without limit or inflict damage on it, we are bound to face its retaliation. China is committed to sustainable development and to the principles of prioritizing resource conservation and environmental protection and letting nature restore itself. We will protect nature and the environment as we do our own lives. We will continue to pursue a model of sound development featuring improved production, higher living standards, and healthy ecosystems to ensure the sustainable development of the Chinese nation.

Critical Reading Skill—Contextualization

Why Contextualization is important for critical reading?

Contextualization is a crucial technique in critical reading that involves understanding and analyzing a text by placing it within its specific historical, cultural, social, or personal context. When you are reading, you need to look for links and connections between the text and your experiences, thoughts, ideas, and other texts. By contextualizing a text, you can better identify the author's purpose, evaluate the text's credibility and relevance, and make informed judgments about its value and significance. For example, when reading a historical document, contextualization involves understanding the document's place in history, the social and political conditions of that time, and how these factors shaped the document's content and perspective. Similarly, when reading a literary text, contextualization can involve understanding the cultural norms and values of the time, which can influence the characters' decisions and the themes of the text.

Tips to train and develop contextualization skill:

(1) Build background knowledge. Read widely, including books, articles, reports, magazines, and etc. to build a broad knowledge base. Understand the historical and cultural contexts in which the text was written to gain insights into the author's perspectives and the societal influences on his/her work.

(2) Analyze textual elements. Identify main idea, purpose and motif of what you read by looking for recurring ideas, symbols, or patterns in the text that connect to its context. Examine the language and style through paying attention to the author's choice of words, tone, and writing style, as these can provide clues about the text's context.

(3) Seek additional resources. Use dictionaries, books, or online resources to clarify unfamiliar words, concepts, or historical events mentioned in the text. Look for scholarly articles, book reviews, or essays that analyze the text and provide alternative interpretations.

(4) Engage in questioning. Challenge the author's assumptions and biases by asking critical questions about the text's content and context. Analyze the author's use of evidence and arguments to support his/her claims, considering the context in which the evidence was presented. Regularly reflect on your reading experiences, considering how the context influenced your understanding of the text.

Warm-up Questions

1. Has the environment in your hometown improved compared with 10 years ago? If yes, in what way has it improved?
2. How do you define Ecological Civilization?
3. What have you contributed to environment protection?

Text

World Day to Combat Desertification and Drought: China's Journey of Pushing Green forward, Desertification back

June 17 marks World Day to Combat Desertification and Drought. As one of the global environmental issues, desertification has serious implications worldwide for biodiversity, eco-safety, poverty eradication, socio-economic stability and sustainable development.

The issue of desertification is not new. However, it is accelerating today, with the degradation of arable land estimated at 30 to 35 times the historical rate, according to the United Nations.

China is one of the countries most affected by desertification in the world. According to the statistics released by China's National Forestry and Grassland Administration in 1998, China had about 2.62 million square kilometers of desertification land, accounting for 27.4 percent of the country's total land area, affecting nearly 400 million people.

Since the 1970s, China has launched several ecological projects such as the Three-North Shelterbelt Forest Program, the Beijing-Tianjin Sandstorm Source Control Project and the control of soil erosion, starting its journey of pushing green forward and desertification back.

After decades of long-term and sustained efforts, the work of combating desertification has yielded positive results. As of 2019, the country had 2.57 million square kilometers of desertification land, a decrease of some 38,000 square kilometers compared with 2014. The area of desertification land has changed from an average annual expansion of over 10,000 square kilometers at the end of the last century to an average annual reduction of more than 2.3 thousand square kilometers today.

Southern edge of Taklimakan Desert turns green

Situated in China's northwest Xinjiang Uyghur Autonomous Region, the Taklimakan Desert is China's largest desert. It's known as the "Sea of Death" because of its harsh environment. As a drifting desert, it could continue expanding.

At the beginning of the 20th century, China began its exploration on desertification control in the region. Local people and scientists have fought against desertification for over 30 years. On both sides of a 565-km road that was built across the desert, more than 20 million trees have been planted.

From the remote sensing images, it can be seen that compared with 2020, the southern edge of the desert in 2022 has become greener because of the planting of more plants.

Green corridors through Kubuqi Desert to protect Yellow River

The Kubuqi Desert, China's seventh-largest desert, is located in the section from Lanzhou Province to Inner Mongolia Autonomous Region of the Yellow River. It is like a basin of sand hanging over the Yellow River, therefore it's very important to manage the desert well to better protect the river.

Since 2012, China has built a 220-kilometer-long green barrier between the Yellow River and the desert to "lock" the sand firmly. The green barrier is a combination of 10 percent trees, 80 percent shrubs, and 10 percent herbs, with a survival rate of more than 80 percent.

"About one-third of the desert area has become green, with 65 percent of the area covered by vegetation, an increase of more than 30 percent from 10 years ago. While the mobile sand has been under control, the ecology of more than 200 kilometers of the Yellow River has been safeguarded," said Wang Wenbiao, secretary-general of Kubuqi International Desert Forum.

The Great Wall of green: Three-North Shelterbelt Forest

In 1978, China launched an ambitious forestation project, the Three-North Shelterbelt Forest Program, in the country's northwest, north and northeast, determined to combat the expanding desert and deteriorating environment.

The project, covering over four million square kilometers, or 42.4 percent of China's land area, is the world's largest forestry ecological project. Over four decades later, conservation efforts have paid off. So far, a total of 320,000 square kilometers of forest has been planted, with the forest coverage rate in the project areas increasing from 5.05 percent in 1978 to 13.84 percent at present. The land area prone to sand dust decreased from 48.1 percent in 2000 to 40.4 percent in 2020.

💡 Glossary

desertification *n.*	荒漠化;沙漠化
biodiversity *n.*	生物多样性
degradation *n.*	恶化,衰退;降解
arable land	耕地
China's National Forestry and Grassland Administration	国家林业和草原局
Three-North Shelterbelt Forest Program	三北防护林工程
the Beijing-Tianjin Sandstorm Source Control Project	京津风沙源治理工程
the control of soil erosion	控制水土流失

💡 Contextualization Reading Tasks

Task 1 Answer Questions.

(1) When you see the title of the text "World Day to Combat Desertification and Drought: China's Journey of Pushing Green forward, Desertification back", what comes to your mind first? And how does it relate to your experience?

(2) What do you think are the key details within the text that can facilitate your understanding of its context? Which areas or places are mentioned and which time periods are referred to, and why are they important to this text?

(3) If you are to add a conclusive paragraph to this text, what will your conclusion look like? Will you consider the broad context of China's environmental governance in your conclusion?

Task 2 Discuss.

Watch the first episode of the TV series *Perfect Youth* (《最美的青春》) and the first episode of the documentary *Desert Oasis Dream* (《大漠绿色梦》), then read Text A again. Discuss the following questions with your group members:

(1) How do the two video materials help you understand Text A?

(2) Are there any differences in your understanding of Text A before and after watching the episodes?

(3) Do you have any personal experience that can help you relate to the text? If yes, what is it?

Text B

China's Green Development in the New Era (Excerpt)

Building the Earth into a Beautiful Home

Green development and eco-environmental progress are the responsibility of all humanity. China has always been a major participant, contributor, and torchbearer in the global movement for building an eco-civilization. It firmly safeguards multilateralism, and is actively forging an international eco-environmental governance pattern in which countries align their interests and share their rights and responsibilities. This is how China does its part in pursuing the sustainable development of humanity.

1. Participating in global climate governance

Following the principles of equity, common but differentiated responsibilities and respective capabilities, China has acted in accordance with the United Nations Framework Convention on Climate Change, actively participated in global climate negotiations in a constructive manner, and made historic contributions to the conclusion and implementation of the Paris Agreement. In doing so, it helps to build a fair, rational, and mutually beneficial global climate governance system.

China has reinforced the effort to achieve its Nationally Determined Contributions (NDCs). It will make the steepest cuts in the world to the intensity of its carbon emissions, and complete the process from carbon emissions peaking to carbon neutrality in the shortest span of time. This fully demonstrates its strong sense of responsibility as a major country.

China is also an active participant in South-South cooperation on climate change. Since 2016, working in other developing countries, it has launched 10 low-carbon demonstration zones, 100 projects for climate change mitigation and adaption, training sessions on climate change response for 1,000 people, and more than 200 foreign assistance programs on climate change.

International cooperation on climate change may encounter difficulties and setbacks, but China will remain committed to improving global climate governance and taking solid actions. As always, it will work with firm resolve towards the goals of carbon emissions peaking and carbon neutrality, actively participate in international cooperation on climate change, engage in international negotiations on climate change in a constructive manner, and do everything in its power to support and assist other developing countries in this realm. In doing so, China will continue to contribute to global efforts to tackle the grave challenge of climate change.

2. Building a green Belt and Road

China is committed to working with other countries on promoting green development under the Belt and Road Initiative (BRI), making it a green initiative. In order to establish a cooperation mechanism for green and low-carbon development under the BRI, China has signed an MoU (Memorandum of Understanding) with the United Nations Environment Programme on building a green Belt and Road, and reached more than 50 cooperation agreements on eco-environmental conservation with relevant countries and international organizations. It has also launched the Initiative for Belt and Road Partnership on Green Development with 31 countries, established the Belt and Road Energy Partnership (BREP) with 32 countries, led the creation of the Belt and Road Initiative International Green Development Coalition (BRIGC), founded the BRI Green Development Institute, and launched the BRI Environmental Big Data Platform.

China has helped other participants in the BRI to build up their environmental governance capacity and improve their people's well-being. It also helps these countries in training personnel for green development, having trained 3,000 people from more than 120 countries under the Green Silk Road Envoys Program. China formulated the Green Investment Principles for the Belt and Road to encourage such investments in related regions. Concurrently, Chinese enterprises have funded renewable energy projects in other BRI countries, and helped them build a number of major clean energy facilities. All these efforts have boosted green development in these countries.

3. Carrying out extensive bilateral and multilateral cooperation

China has taken active steps to advance practical cooperation on saving resources and protecting the eco-environment. It successfully hosted the first part of the 15th meeting of the Conference of the Parties to the Convention on Biological Diversity (COP15) and the 14th meeting of the Conference of the Contracting Parties to the Ramsar Convention on Wetlands.

China is an active participant in cooperation on energy transition and energy efficiency under the frameworks of G20, China-ASEAN partnership, ASEAN Plus Three, East Asia Summit, Forum on China-Africa Cooperation, BRICS, Shanghai Cooperation Organization, and Asia-Pacific Economic Cooperation (APEC). It took the lead in formulating the G20 Energy Efficiency Leading Programme, a key outcome of the G20 Hangzhou Summit. It has put into action the Global Development Initiative, and worked for the establishment of the Global Clean Energy Cooperation Partnership.

China has also carried out cooperation with other countries and regions—including India, Brazil, South Africa, the United States, Japan, Germany, France, and ASEAN countries—in the fields of energy conservation, environmental protection, clean energy, response to climate change, biodiversity protection, prevention and control of desertification, and conservation of marine and forest resources.

China also supports international organizations, including the UN agencies, Asian Development Bank, Asian Infrastructure Investment Bank, New Development Bank, Global Environment Facility, Green Climate Fund, International Energy Agency, and International Renewable Energy Agency, in carrying out technological assistance, capacity building and trial programs for green and low-carbon development in key sectors such as industry, agriculture, energy, transport, and urban-rural development. Through these efforts China has made a significant contribution to advancing sustainable development worldwide.

Conclusion

China has embarked on a new journey to build itself into a modern socialist country in all respects and advance the rejuvenation of the Chinese nation. Harmony between humanity and nature is an important feature of China's modernization.

The just-concluded 20th CPC National Congress has made strategic plans for China's future development which will help to create a better environment with greener mountains, cleaner water, and clearer air. China will keep to the path of green development, continue to build an eco-civilization, and strive to realize development with a higher level of quality, efficiency, equity, sustainability and security. We will make "green" a defining feature of a beautiful China and allow the people to share the beauty of nature and life in a healthy environment.

The earth is our one and only home, and humanity and nature form a community of life. It is the common responsibility of all countries to protect the environment and promote sustainable development. China stands ready to work with the international community to advance eco-environmental conservation, promote green development, protect the green earth, and build a cleaner and more beautiful world.

💡 Glossary

align *v.*	公开支持,与……结盟
equity *n.*	公平,公正
United Nations Framework Convention on Climate Change	联合国气候变化框架公约
Nationally Determined Contributions	国家自主贡献
carbon neutrality	碳中和,一般指国家、企业、个人等在一定时间内直接或间接产生的二氧化碳或温室气体排放总量,通过植树造林、节能减排等形式,以抵消自身排放量,达到相对"零排放"
MoU	谅解备忘录(Memorandum of Understanding)
Conference of the Parties to the Convention on Biological Diversity	生物多样性公约缔约方会议

💡 Contextualization Reading Tasks

Task 1 Decide whether the following statements are TRUE or FALSE.

(1)(   ) China has actively participated in global climate negotiations and has made significant contributions to various agreements.

(2)(   ) China's green development is set against the context of building itself into a modern socialist country in all respects and advance the rejuvenation of the Chinese nation.

(3) (   ) China's green development strategy aims to transform the entire planet into a beautiful home.

(4) (   ) The Chinese government has implemented strict environmental regulations to protect the natural environment.

(5) (   ) The Chinese government has set ambitious targets for carbon reduction and renewable energy usage.

(6) (   ) China's green development initiatives have not received international recognition or support.

Task 2　Make a presentation.

Please work with your group members to research on "United Nations Framework Convention on Climate Change" and "Paris Agreement". Find out what the two agreements are and what they have to do with China. Then make a presentation to the class on China's role in the above-mentioned agreements.

Voice beyond Borders

Text C

Earth Day a Reminder of Our Shared Obligation①

April 22 is Earth Day and people all around the world will be celebrating the bounties that earth provides for all life. This is a good time to consider what does living "a green life" mean to us? How can we live green from a holistic systems perspective? China's pursuit of an "ecological civilization", an enabling philosophy for green life, is now written into the Chinese Constitution as the basis for the country's environmental policies, laws and education. It articulates the primary principles of environmental management, ecological restoration and green development. It has deep cultural roots in Lao Tzu's Taoist notion of "uniting humans and the universe". So we look to China for leadership in accomplishing this vision of nature-human harmony.

This harmony implies preserving the places we love and making our own behaviors, particularly consumption, more mindful and intentional, while transforming the infrastructural systems that we live in.

We can be preserving places both far and near to us. About eight years ago I visited the city of Xiamen and sat by the seaside enjoying the beautiful ocean views and mild weather. It changed my impression of China, which was originally formed by visits to crowded and busy Beijing and Shanghai. China has many amazingly beautiful places worth preserving—the Zhangjiajie Floating peaks, the Lijiang River, the Great Wall, Mount Qomolangma, Tiger Leaping Gorge on the Yangtze River, the Yarlung Tsangpo Grand Canyon, among many others. But on Earth Day, the most amazing places to focus on are our own backyards, our neighborhoods, our community spaces.

---

① The author of the text is Paul Shrivastava, co-president of the Club of Rome and professor at Pennsylvania State University.

There is great potential for treating these local spaces with greater respect, keeping them clean and green, even improving their biodiversity with new plantings and establishing pollinator and bird habitats. Many communities are experimenting with converting impersonal urban spaces into more social community places, by planting trees or bushes in unused lots, in back alleys, in parking areas, creating farmers' markets, rooftop farms and vertical farming, and repurposing abandoned or underutilized buildings for community activities.

We should focus on changing human behaviors. Earth Day is a reminder that Earth systems today are more impacted by human social and economic behaviors than by natural processes and cycles. We are living in a time when human activities dominate the natural hydrological, carbon and nitrogen cycles. How can we make human impacts less harmful to nature? Yes, part of the answer is reducing consumption, but that is only a partial answer that applies mostly to wealthy people. People can do a lot to improve their own consumption behaviors, by reducing waste, recycling, sharing rather than buying, walking, cycling to work, and avoiding single-use plastics. A more encompassing way to moderate our collective impacts on earth is to become more mindful and intentional in all that we do.

Human self-actualization and happiness are not all about consumption. Humans are an integral part of nature, and we must come to see ourselves in this unitary way. There are many ways of being human in relation to our environments.

Mindfulness and intentionality open possibilities of satisfaction, finding meaning and happiness, while reducing the material impacts. They can diffuse our focus from material acquisition and consumption, to spiritual, psychic, social and transcendent satisfactions. Mindful activities can rejuvenate community, kinship and joy through connection and empathy. Many people are adopting tai chi, yoga, meditation, journaling, deep-listening, expressing gratitude, reading, silence and other contemplative practices to find purpose and meaning in life. These practices can have profound influence on improving individual's well-being and self-esteem and deflecting from habitual consumptive behaviors.

Green living by individuals depends on the availability of green infrastructures and systems. There are limits to how much individual personal changes can improve Earth systems. Many impacts are determined by the systems and infrastructures that surround us, systems that supply electricity, water and food, transportation, healthcare and education. Many of these systems are aging and were designed in times of older and less efficient technologies. They are often just taken for granted. We don't personally own them, so they drop out of sight and out of mind.

Earth Day is a good time to remind us of our responsibilities toward making these lifestyle enabling systems to be ecologically efficient and regenerative of life on earth. Regenerative agriculture, renewable energy, nature-based infrastructure are ways of ensuring the long-term conservation of Earth systems and ecological services. Citizens can influence these systems by demanding such green systems. They can engage the government institutions, corporations and nongovernmental organizations responsible for maintaining such services.

Citizen engagement in civic decision-making is a potent way for systems transformation toward sustainability. Positive approaches to engagement can enrich local government bodies with innovative ideas, understanding of their clients' needs and opportunities for collaboration. Citizen engagement is also a way to ensuring that the benefits of green infrastructure are distributed in a socially just and inclusive manner.

Working toward a holistic systemic green life is a worthy way of celebrating Earth Day this year and every year. If pursued collectively, it can slow down the global collapse of ecosystems and climate change. A green lifestyle can bring joy and connection to nature and connection to neighbors and communities. Let us not just watch and lament the devastation to nature that we witness every day.

There is a lot that we can act on locally, and small acts accumulate to big changes. Let us act in small and local ways as a Chinese proverb advises: "Before preparing to improve the world first look around your own home three times."

Glossary

bounty *n.*	慷慨,丰富
holistic *adj.*	整体的,全面的
articulate *v.*	清楚地说明
unite humans and the universe	天人合一
pollinator *n.*	传粉者,传粉媒介
hydrological *adj.*	水文学的
nitrogen *n.*	氮
self-actualization	自我实现
unitary *adj.*	单一的;统一的

diffuse v. 扩散,弥漫;减弱

transcendent *adj.* 卓越的;超常的;出类拔萃的

deflecting *adj.* 偏转的;变向的

potent *adj.* 强大的,有力的

Contextualization Reading Tasks

Task 1 Answer questions.

(1) What is the motif of the text?
(2) Can you find any clues about the readership the author is writing for?
(3) What additional resources did you consult to help you better understand the context?

Task 2 Make a speech.

The author has suggested that we can act in small and local ways to help protect the earth. Please make a 3-minute speech on the following topic "Small Acts Big Changes".

Practical Assignment

1. **Conduct research on one of the following topics:**
   (1) plastic pollution on campus
   (2) high quality development of Yellow River basin
   (3) straw checkerboard barrier in Shapotou, Zhongwei City, Ningxia

   Find out how your selected topic affects our life. You can collect the data by searching the Internet, interviewing related person or expert, making a field trip, consulting teachers or students from the Department of Ecology and Environment in your university. Then analyze your data and come up with a report on your findings.

2. **Carbon footprint survey**

   A carbon footprint is historically defined as "the total set of greenhouse gas (GHG) emissions caused by an organization, event, product or person". Please conduct a detailed survey of your carbon footprint and find out what you can do to offset your carbon emission. Share with the whole class how we can change our way of life, transforming from "high carbon" life to "low carbon" life.

 Additional Resources

Digital Resource 5-1

Unit 6

Law

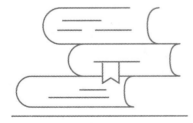

二十大报告选摘

Report to the 20th National Congress of the Communist Party of China (Excerpt)

全面依法治国是国家治理的一场深刻革命,关系党执政兴国,关系人民幸福安康,关系党和国家长治久安。必须更好发挥法治固根本、稳预期、利长远的保障作用,在法治轨道上全面建设社会主义现代化国家。

The comprehensive advancement of law-based governance has been a profound revolution in China's governance. Law-based governance is important for the Party's success in governing and rejuvenating the country, for the wellbeing of the people, and for the long-term stability of the Party and the country. We must give better play to the role of the rule of law in consolidating foundations, ensuring stable expectations, and delivering long-term benefits, and we must strive to build a modern socialist country in all respects under the rule of law.

公正司法是维护社会公平正义的最后一道防线。深化司法体制综合配套改革,全面准确落实司法责任制,加快建设公正高效权威的社会主义司法制度,努力让人民群众在每一个司法案件中感受到公平正义。规范司法权力运行,健全公安机关、检察机关、审判机关、司法行政机关各司其职、相互配合、相互制约的体制机制。强化对司法活动的制约监督,促进司法公正。加强检察机关法律监督工作。完善公益诉讼制度。

An impartial judiciary is the last line of defense for social fairness and justice. We will deepen comprehensive and integrated reform of the judicial system, fully and faithfully enforce judicial accountability, and accelerate the development of a fair, efficient, and authoritative socialist judicial system. We will see that the people feel justice has been served in each and every judicial case.

We will ensure the well-regulated exercise of judicial power and improve the systems and mechanisms that enable public security organs, procuratorates, courts, and administrative agencies for justice to perform their respective functions and to coordinate with and check one another. Checks and oversight on judicial activities will be enhanced to ensure judicial justice. Procuratorial organs will step up legal oversight, and the system of public-interest litigation will be improved.

Critical Reading Skill—Synthesizing

What is synthesizing important for critical reading?

To synthesize is to combine ideas and create a completely new idea. That new idea becomes the conclusion you have drawn from your reading. It causes you to weigh ideas, to compare, judge, think, and explore—and then to arrive at a moment that you haven't known before. You begin with simple summary, work through analysis, evaluate using critique, and then move on to synthesis. Instead of just restating the important points from text, synthesizing involves combining ideas and allowing an evolving understanding of text. It is also defined as creating original insights, perspectives, and understandings by reflecting on text(s) and merging elements from text and existing schema. To make it simpler, synthesizing is to put pieces together to see them in a new way.

It is an important critical reading skill, as it involves the ability to combine information from various sources to create a new understanding or perspective on a topic. When reading complex texts, synthesizing allows you to analyze, interpret, and evaluate information from different sources. Suppose you have read several articles on China's rule of law from different sources, each offering a unique perspective on the topic. Let's see how synthesizing may help you.

(1) Identify themes. As you read the articles, you come across discussions about China's legal reforms, including efforts to strengthen the judiciary, enhance legal transparency, and promote the protection of individual rights. You also encounter articles that highlight specific cases or legislative changes aimed at advancing the rule of law in China.

(2) Recognize diverse perspectives. Each article presents different viewpoints, such as legal experts analyzing the impact of specific reforms, multinational corporations and investors seeking a transparent and predictable legal environment that protects their investments, ensures fair competition, and upholds contractual rights and government officials outlining the rationale behind legal initiatives.

(3) Make connections. Through synthesizing, you begin to connect the information

across the articles. For example, you might notice how recent legal reforms align with China's broader economic and social development goals, as well as how specific court cases reflect evolving interpretations of legal principles. You also recognize the challenges and criticisms raised by observers regarding the enforcement of laws and protection of individual rights.

(4) Form a comprehensive understanding. By synthesizing the information from these diverse sources, you develop a more comprehensive understanding of China's progress in the rule of law. You are able to see the interplay between legal reforms, societal dynamics, and international perspectives on China's legal system.

(5) Develop informed perspectives. With this synthesized understanding, you can form your own informed perspective on China's progress in the rule of law. You may be better equipped to critically evaluate the complexities of legal developments in China, engage in discussions about the rule of law, and contribute to informed analyses of China's legal system and its implications domestically and internationally.

Warm-up Questions

1. What makes a fair and just society?
2. Why is law-based governance so important to China?
3. What is the rule of virtue?

Text

China's Law-Based Cyberspace Governance in the New Era (Excerpt)

Defending Fairness and Justice in Cyberspace

An impartial judiciary is the last line of defense for social fairness and justice. China has stayed committed to the principle of maintaining judicial justice and administrating justice for the people. Actively responding to the needs of justice in the age of Internet, China has employed Internet and information technology to empower the traditional judiciary, improved rules of cyber justice, and reformed models of cyber justice. This has allowed it to settle new types of cyber disputes in accordance with the law, combat cybercrime, safeguard the rights and interests of cyberspace players, and deliver judicial services that are more fair, just, open, transparent, efficient, accessible, inclusive, and equitable.

1. Defining New Rules of Cyber Justice

As new Internet technologies, applications and business forms develop quickly, legal relationships in cyberspace are becoming more diverse, posing new challenges to the administration of justice in cyberspace. This calls for better-defined rules of cyber justice.

For this purpose, China has produced timely judicial interpretations of civil and criminal issues such as intellectual property rights, the right to dignity, online transactions, and unfair competition on the Internet, as well as telecom and online fraud. It has handled a good number of unprecedented, complicated cases that are closely related to the Internet, such as those involving Internet infrastructure security, algorithms, data rights and trading, protection of personal information, and management of online platforms. In the process, it has refined the criteria for the application of the law and made the standards for adjudication consistent. This has led to increasing clarity on the rules, code of conduct, and boundaries of rights, obligations and responsibilities in cyberspace. China has formulated rules for online litigation, mediation and operation of the people's courts, refined rules on taking electronic data as evidence, and standardized the procedures for handling cybercrime cases. As a result, a system of rules and procedures for cyber justice is taking shape. This systematic development of relevant rules provides regulatory guidance and institutional safeguards for cyber justice, which is therefore becoming more rule-based.

2. Exploring New Models of Cyber Justice

China has been active in exploring new channels, domains and models for further integrating Internet technology with judicial activities, for the purpose of speedier delivery of justice. In order to build a cyber justice model with Chinese characteristics, it has piloted measures in applying the latest technologies such as big data, cloud computing, artificial intelligence and blockchain in judicial proceedings, judgment enforcement, judicial administration, and other fields.

Local courts are encouraged to explore new mechanisms with regional features for Internet-empowered adjudication, on the basis of the development of local Internet industry and the characteristics of local cyber disputes. Internet courts have been established in Hangzhou, Beijing and Guangzhou, in an attempt to realize adjudication of Internet-related cases via the Internet. In the process of digitalizing procuratorial work, China has used big data to empower legal oversight. It has systematically integrated a wide range of case information, worked on models and platforms for big data-based legal oversight, and implemented oversight of the prosecution of individual cases and of similar cases in order to address the common problems they raise. This has helped improve the quality and efficiency of legal oversight in the new era. The emergence of these new models signifies the further development of a socialist judicial system with Chinese characteristics in cyberspace, and is becoming a salient feature of China's judicial system.

3. Judicial Protection of Online Rights and Interests

China has carried out judicial activities to combat cybercrime, so that the people can see that justice is served in every judicial case.

Strengthen judicial protection of online civil rights and interests. To protect the online civil rights and interests of all parties concerned, China handles civil and commercial cases involving personal information, intellectual property rights, online transactions, and online infringement in accordance with the law. For protection of personal information, the focus is put on online platforms that process huge amounts of personal information. Civil public-interest litigations have been launched against online platforms suspected of abusing personal information. In adjudicating these cases, the courts have clarified the rules and limits for the commercial use of customers' personal information, and prompted companies running online platforms to collect and use data in accordance with laws and regulations. For protection of intellectual property rights in Internet-related cases of high technological complexity such as those involving patents, integrated circuit designs, technological secrets, and computer software, the courts have introduced a technology investigator system. Step by step, safeguards are being set up in cyberspace to protect citizens' legitimate rights and interests there.

Intensify punishment for cybercrime. As Internet technology evolves swiftly, conventional crimes are transforming rapidly into Internet-enabled, no-contact forms, leading to a rise in illicit acts such as telecom and online fraud, online gambling, and online pornography. China handles new types of cybercrime in accordance with the law. In recent years China has carried out a systematic "Internet clean-up" campaign, combating cyber hacking, invasion of individual privacy, and many other criminal acts that cause strong concern to the public. It has launched a number of campaigns against telecom and online fraud, including those to hunt fugitives via cloud services and platforms, freeze the SIM cards and bank accounts used by suspects, intercept domestic recruitment by criminal groups operating from abroad, and pursue the heads and key members of criminal groups. It combats all types of predatory lending including trap loans, the student loan, reverse mortgage, and elder investment scams. It punishes in accordance with the law the shadowy businesses that provide services such as Internet connection, domain registration, server hosting, mobile application development, online payment, and promotion to criminal groups behind telecom and online fraud.

China has also updated its national anti-fraud big data platform and anti-fraud app, built a national fraud database, and improved the mechanisms for quick freezing of payments and retrieval of swindled money. It takes resolute action against online gambling and delivers harsh punishments for online pornography. Through these efforts, remarkable progress has been made in combating cybercrime, giving the people a stronger sense of security and reinforcing social harmony and stability.

Explore new avenues for judicial protection of minors in cyberspace. While focusing on forestalling and punishing cybercrime, China takes targeted measures against online criminal activities such as virtual sexual harassment, and has increased punishments for those preying on minors. Through law-based punishment and individualized assistance and education, the state does its utmost to rehabilitate underage people involved in cybercrime. China has strengthened the protection of minors in cyberspace, making breakthroughs in typical cases such as those concerning circulation of audio and video about narcotics, violation of minors' personal information rights and interests, and excessive livestream rewards from minor viewers. By taking action in the form of public-interest litigation, written suggestions from prosecutorial organizations, support for prosecutions, and briefings on relevant information, China is working to pool the strength of online platforms, the public, and the government to foster a healthy cyber environment for young people.

Glossary

litigation *n.*	诉讼,起诉
adjudication *n.*	裁定;判决
procuratorial *adj.*	代理人的;代诉的
infringement *n.*	(对他人权益的)侵犯;(对法律、规则等的)违反,违背
"Internet clean-up" campaign	净网行动
fugitive *n.*	逃亡者
intercept *v.*	拦截,阻截
prey on	捕食;掠夺

Text B

Judicial Reform Promotes Rule of Law[①]

China's recent efforts to reform the legal and judicial system, in order to promote more effective rule of law reflect its longstanding commitment to pursue modernization and foster a rules-based society. All this is embodied in the resolution the recent Sixth Plenary Session of the 19th Central Committee of the Communist Party of China issued.

For those of us working directly with legal practitioners on the ground in China for the past three decades, we have witnessed this evolution and advancement first hand. Professionalizing the judiciary not only makes courts more trustworthy and respectable in the eyes of the people, but also enhances its capability to resolve disputes, and thus contributes to a more vibrant, prosperous community.

The upgrading of the legal regime also reflects the realities of a sophisticated market economy, catalyzing the communal accumulation of shared wealth. The growth of the market and the massive increase in consumer transactions which take place as society advances mean a potential increase in commercial disputes, and highlight the necessity of having a strong rule of law apparatus in place. As China has become an increasingly important commercial and trading country over the past few decades, a more professional judicial system will help it to undergird stable, robust economic relations with other global powers.

In this manner, China's economic growth combined with the advancement of the rule of law can help contribute to the stability of the global financial system, which becomes all the more important in these times of a deeply interconnected world still recovering from the economic impacts of the COVID-19 pandemic.

Yet since China was the first major economy to recover from the impacts of the pandemic, the momentum could add to its economic stability.

The commitment to foster a society ruled by law has manifested itself in concrete actions taken on the ground. Specifically, recent Chinese policy initiatives have ensured that a judge

---

① This article was issued in 2021.

hearing a case will be responsible for its outcome too, which in fact is incentivizing superior quality trial management. And the judge quota protocols ensure that only the most qualified individuals occupy the prestigious post of a judge.

Besides, the implementation of a Civil Code on Jan 1 this year, the first since the founding of the People's Republic of China, is a major step toward compiling a single codified source of civil law that will simplify both research and understanding.

Also, the funding of judicial bodies has largely been moved to the provincial level and above, eliminating the possibility of corrupt local officials interfering with the fair and proper adjudication of disputes.

In certain technological and functional areas, China has outpaced many Western countries in pioneering courts to deal with diverse issues, even paving the way for blockchain technology to be used to help authenticate evidence that will be used at a trial.

As for the pandemic, it has accelerated the shift toward digitalization, resulting in a far greater degree of procedural steps being handled online and bringing convenience to litigants, who don't necessarily have to travel long distances to be physically present in a court for their case. On issues such as intellectual property and data protection—which are crucial in a digitalized economy—China has implemented legislation that will ensure all parties' rights are protected and concerns addressed.

China has in recent years further expanded the realm of legal education, including starting a Constitution week and leading initiatives that allow people to learn more about how legal bodies function. These measures will help foster stability, allowing the intellectual property space to continue to rapidly expand.

In certain other domains, China has been able to learn from the experience and systems of other countries and, in some cases, applying them to its own unique context, creating a rule of law with Chinese characteristics. This approach can help to mitigate the chances of laws becoming stagnant or too formulaic to handle real problems, and maintain the focus on practicality and substance over form.

Many public opinion surveys have shown that these undertakings have resulted in growing trust in the competence of the judiciary, and more people becoming familiar with the process of trials and the reasoning used in court verdicts, which is very important because it plays a vital role in losing parties retaining their faith in the judicial system.

The importance of the rule of law cannot be overstated, as it is a fundamental feature of any well-functioning society. Therefore, China's commitment to promote the rule of law should be reassuring not only for the Chinese people, but also for the world as a whole.

💡 Glossary

Sixth Plenary Session of the 19th Central Committee of the Communist Party of China	党的十九届六中全会
judicial *adj.*	法庭的,司法的
practitioner *n.*	(医学界或法律界的)从业人员,执业者
catalyze *v.*	催化;刺激,促进
communal *adj.*	公共的;群体的,团体的
apparatus *n.*	设备,器具
undergird *v.*	加强;从底层加固
momentum *n.*	动力,势头
incentivize *v.*	有奖鼓励,激励
quota *n.*	(候选人当选所需的)规定票数,最低票数
Civil Code	民法典:一套系统的法律规定,涉及私人之间的交易,如商业合同和过失诉讼等
litigant *n.*	诉讼当事人
mitigate *v.*	减轻,缓和
stagnant *adj.*	(经济、社会等)停滞不前的,不景气的
formulaic *adj.*	公式化的;刻板的

Voice beyond Borders

Text C

International Law for the Global Community of Shared Future[①]

On September 26, 2023, the State Council Information Office published an elaborated white paper entitled "A Global Community of Shared Future (GCSF): China's Proposals and Actions." The concept was first mentioned by Chinese President Xi Jinping in 2013, when addressing the audience at the Moscow State Institute of International Relations.

In 2018, the GCSF concept was included in the preamble of the People's Republic of China's Constitution. This preamble now declares among others that "The achievements of China's revolution, development and reform would have been impossible without the support of the world's people. The future of China is closely bound up with the future of the world." The inclusion of the GCSF concept in the country's foundational legal document not only underscores the importance of this concept but also the leadership and responsibility that China is willing to assume in global affairs. The State Council's white paper further elaborates the guiding principles of the GCSF and demonstrates how China's GCSF proposal is grounded in international law.

The GCSF white paper builds on the existing international law regimes, while at the same time offering new ideas and directions for their reform. Highlighting the fact that the world is currently facing multiple governance crises, the white paper calls for resolving emerging global problems through international cooperation. This cooperation should be based on the *UN Charter*, which in Article 2 affirms the principles of territorial integrity, sovereign equality, and non-interference in internal affairs.

---

① The author of the text is Alexandr Svetlicinii, an Associate Professor of law at the University of Macau, where he also serves as program coordinator for the Master of Law in International Business Law in English Language.

In line with these principles, China's GCSF vision rejects the pursuit of global hegemony by individual countries through the containment of "rising powers". It equally rejects the "universal values" defined by a handful of countries and lacking "universal acceptance" by others. Instead, the GCSF promotes consensus-based cooperation among sovereign states in line with the aforementioned principles contained in the *UN Charter* and affirmed in the Five Principles of Peaceful Coexistence proposed at the Bandung Conference in 1955.

Reflecting the growing discontent of many states with the current state of compliance with international law, the GCSF white paper emphasizes the need to strive for equity and justice in international affairs. These objectives, likewise, could be achieved by safeguarding the international order based on international law, upholding the authority of the international rule of law, and ensuring equal and unified application of international law.

China has continuously opposed unilateral economic sanctions, which frequently contravene existing rules of international trade. Unfortunately, due to the blocking of the appointment process, the World Trade Organization's (WTO) dispute settlement mechanism remains dysfunctional and cannot resolve ongoing trade disputes, frequently caused by protectionist trade restrictions veiled as security-related measures. On September 27, at the group study session of the Political Bureau of the CPC Central Committee, President Xi once again called for the restoration of the normal operation of the WTO dispute settlement mechanism.

The realization of the GCSF vision will require extensive cooperation and consensus-building in international relations. China has demonstrated its support for consensus decision-making as exemplified in its work with BRICS. BRICS has accepted several new member countries to join in 2024, which conveys the attractiveness of this cooperation mode, especially for developing countries. The New Development Bank established by the BRICS in 2014 is also based on the equality of members in the decision-making process, which presents an alternative to other development organizations dominated by the large donor countries.

The GCSF is an ambitious vision that merits attention of the global community of nations. The commonly shared objectives of this vision would need to be embedded in international law instruments to ensure compliance and effective implementation. As a result, it could serve as a much-needed impetus to trigger the long-expected reforms in the existing international law structures that should better reflect the diversity of states and their shared interest in peaceful development.

Glossary

preamble *n.*	(法规、契约的)序言,绪论;前言
territorial integrity	领土完整
sovereign equality	主权平等
non-interference in internal affairs	不干涉内政
compliance *n.*	服从,遵守;屈从,迁就;可塑性
unilateral economic sanctions	单边经济制裁
contravene *v.*	抵触;违反;反驳;否认

Synthesizing Reading Tasks

Task 1 Answer questions.

(1) What is the central theme or idea that ties all three articles together? How does each article contribute to this overarching theme?

(2) How does the perspective of the second text differ from the other two?

(3) Compare and contrast the legal frameworks discussed in "China's Law-Based Cyberspace Governance in the New Era" and "International Law for the Global Community of Shared Future". What are the similarities and differences in their approaches to law and governance?

Task 2 Create a diagram.

Create a diagram or a table comparing the key elements of each article's focus, including their perspectives on the role of law and their implications and impact domestically and internationally.

Task 3 Analyze.

Read the following articles from the Criminal Law of the People's Republic of China, analyze the consideration behind these Articles.

Article 17

If a person who has reached the age of 16 commits a crime, he shall bear criminal responsibility.

If a person who has reached the age of 14 but not the age of 16 commits intentional homicide, intentionally hurts another person so as to cause serious injury or death of the person, or commits rape, robbery, drug trafficking, arson, explosion or poisoning, he shall bear criminal responsibility.

If a person who has reached the age of 14 but not the age of 18 commits a crime, he shall be given a lighter or mitigated punishment.

Article 19

Any deaf-mute or blind person who commits a crime may be given a lighter or mitigated punishment or be exempted from punishment.

Article 20

An act that a person commits to stop an unlawful infringement in order to prevent the interests of the State and the public, or his own or other person's rights of the person, property or other rights from being infringed upon by the on-going infringement, thus harming the perpetrator, is justifiable defense, and he shall not bear criminal responsibility.

If a person's act of justifiable defense obviously exceeds the limits of necessity and causes serious damage, he shall bear criminal responsibility; however, he shall be given a mitigated punishment or be exempted from punishment.

If a person acts in defense against an on-going assault, murder, robbery, rape, kidnap or any other crime of violence that seriously endangers his personal safety, thus causing injury or death to the perpetrator of the unlawful act, it is not undue defense, and he shall not bear criminal responsibility.

Practical Assignment

1. Please select a recent legal case in China that highlights the application of the rule of law. Analyze the case thoroughly, discussing the legal framework, the process of adjudication, and the outcome. Evaluate the effectiveness of the legal system in handling the case and upholding the principles of the rule of law.

2. Conduct thorough research on the evolution of China's legal system, focusing on key reforms and legislative changes. Analyze the role of the Communist Party of China (CPC) in shaping the legal system and promoting the rule of law. Identify major legal institutions and their functions in upholding the rule of law.

Additional Resources

Digital Resource 6-1

Unit 7

Science and Technology

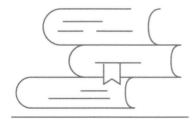

二十大报告选摘

Report to the 20th National Congress of the Communist Party of China (Excerpt)

教育、科技、人才是全面建设社会主义现代化国家的基础性、战略性支撑。必须坚持科技是第一生产力、人才是第一资源、创新是第一动力,深入实施科教兴国战略、人才强国战略、创新驱动发展战略,开辟发展新领域新赛道,不断塑造发展新动能新优势。

Education, science and technology, and human resources are the foundational and strategic pillars for building a modern socialist country in all respects. We must regard science and technology as our primary productive force, talent as our primary resource, and innovation as our primary driver of growth. We will fully implement the strategy for invigorating China through science and education, the workforce development strategy, and the innovation-driven development strategy. We will open up new areas and new arenas in development and steadily foster new growth drivers and new strengths.

我们要坚持教育优先发展、科技自立自强、人才引领驱动,加快建设教育强国、科技强国、人才强国,坚持为党育人、为国育才,全面提高人才自主培养质量,着力造就拔尖创新人才,聚天下英才而用之。

We will continue to give high priority to the development of education, build China's self-reliance and strength in science and technology, and rely on talent to pioneer and to propel development. We will speed up work to build a strong educational system, greater scientific and technological strength, and a quality workforce. We will continue efforts to cultivate talent for the Party and the country and comprehensively improve our ability to nurture talent at home. All this will see us producing first-class innovators and attracting the brightest minds from all over.

Critical Reading Skill—Inference

Why is inference important for critical reading?

Inference involves making logical deductions and conclusions based on the information provided in a text, rather than directly stated. This skill goes beyond simply understanding the surface meaning of the words and sentences and requires you to engage deeply with the text, drawing on contextual cues, characters' behaviors and motivations, as well as your own life experiences. This skill enables you to gain a deeper understanding of the text and connect it to real-world situations. Take Text A in this unit as an example: China calls on all countries to enhance information exchange and technological cooperation on the governance of AI; it put forward some suggestions. The following is an excerpted sentence from the first suggestion, and one inference of this sentence is provided for you to better understand this skill.

Example: We should uphold a people-centered approach in developing AI...

Inference: The development of AI should prioritize the needs, interests, and welfare of people. It suggests that AI should not be developed solely for technological or economic gain, but should be designed and implemented in a way that benefits society and its members.

Justification: The use of the phrase "people-centered approach" suggests that the focus should be on ensuring that AI technologies are designed and implemented with the best interests of people in mind. This means decisions about AI should not be made solely based on technological or economic factors, but should also consider the social, ethical and human impacts.

More inferences can be made from the example sentence than the one stated. You can try to come up with some other inferences based on the clues.

Tips to train and develop inference skill:

(1) Identify clues. When trying to make an inference, it's important to look for clues

that will help you figure out what's going on. Look for key details, examples, comparisons, contrasts, the author's identity, tone or choice of words or the story's setting. These can provide hints or clues to help you make inferences.

(2) Connect the dots. Making an inference is like connecting the dots between the clues you find. It would be best to look for patterns and connections between different pieces of information to help you understand what's happening.

(3) Use your own experience. Sometimes, the best way to make an inference is to use your experience. For example, Text C in this unit is about Xiaomi, the mobile phone, you can think about what you know of Xiaomi or smart phones in general and compare what you read of Xiaomi from the text with your own use of mobile phone.

(4) Consider different viewpoints. Inferences require you to think about different perspectives. This means trying to see things from the point of view of other people and thinking about how their experiences and beliefs might affect their decisions.

(5) Be flexible. Making reasonable inferences means being willing to change your mind as you get more information. It's important to be open to different explanations and interpretations of what's happening and to be willing to change your initial idea or assumption as you learn more.

Warm-up Questions

1. Which technology interests you most, and why?
2. In which science and technology area(s) is China leading the world?
3. What are the advantages and disadvantages that science and technology have brought to humans?

Text A

Global AI Governance Initiative

Artificial intelligence (AI) is a new area of human development. Currently, the fast development of AI around the globe has exerted profound influence on socioeconomic development and the progress of human civilization, and brought huge opportunities to the world. However, AI technologies also bring about unpredictable risks and complicated challenges. The governance of AI, a common task faced by all countries in the world, bears on the future of humanity.

As global peace and development faces various challenges, all countries should commit to a vision of common, comprehensive, cooperative, and sustainable security, and put equal emphasis on development and security. Countries should build consensus through dialogue and cooperation, and develop open, fair, and efficient governing mechanisms, in a bid to promote AI technologies to benefit humanity and contribute to building a community with a shared future for mankind.

We call on all countries to enhance information exchange and technological cooperation on the governance of AI. We should work together to prevent risks, and develop AI governance frameworks, norms and standards based on broad consensus, so as to make AI technologies more secure, reliable, controllable, and equitable. We welcome governments, international organizations, companies, research institutes, civil organizations, and individuals to jointly promote the governance of AI under the principles of extensive consultation, joint contribution, and shared benefits.

To make this happen, we would like to suggest the following.

We should uphold a people-centered approach in developing AI, with the goal of increasing the wellbeing of humanity and on the premise of ensuring social security and respecting the rights and interests of humanity, so that AI always develops in a way that is beneficial to human civilization. We should actively support the role of AI in promoting sustainable development and tackling global challenges such as climate change and biodiversity conservation.

We should respect other countries' national sovereignty and strictly abide by their laws when providing them with AI products and services. We oppose using AI technologies for the purposes of manipulating public opinion, spreading disinformation, intervening in other countries' internal affairs, social systems and social order, as well as jeopardizing the sovereignty of other states.

We must adhere to the principle of developing AI for good, respect the relevant international laws, and align AI development with humanity's common values of peace, development, equity, justice, democracy, and freedom. We should work together to prevent and fight against the misuse and malicious use of AI technologies by terrorists, extreme forces, and transnational organized criminal groups. All countries, especially major countries, should adopt a prudent and responsible attitude to the research, development, and application of AI technologies in the military field.

We should uphold the principles of mutual respect, equality, and mutual benefit in AI development. All countries, regardless of their size, strength, or social system, should have equal rights to develop and use AI. We call for global collaboration to foster the sound development of AI, share AI knowledge, and make AI technologies available to the public under open-source terms. We oppose drawing ideological lines or forming exclusive groups to obstruct other countries from developing AI. We also oppose creating barriers and disrupting the global AI supply chain through technological monopolies and unilateral coercive measures.

We should promote the establishment of a testing and assessment system based on AI risk levels, implement agile governance, and carry out tiered and category-based management for rapid and effective response. R&D entities should improve the explainability and predictability of AI, increase data authenticity and accuracy, ensure that AI always remains under human control, and build trustworthy AI technologies that can be reviewed, monitored, and traced.

We should gradually establish and improve relevant laws, regulations and rules, and ensure personal privacy and data security in the R&D and application of AI. We oppose theft, tampering, leaking, and other illegal collection and use of personal information.

We should adhere to the principles of fairness and non-discrimination, and avoid biases and discrimination based on ethnicities, beliefs, nationalities, genders, etc., during the process of data collection, algorithm design, technology development, and product development and application.

We should put ethics first. We should establish and improve ethical principles, norms, and accountability mechanisms for AI, formulate AI ethical guidelines, and build sci-tech ethical review and regulatory system. We should clarify responsibilities and power boundaries for entities related to AI, fully respect and safeguard the legitimate rights and interests of various groups, and address domestic and international ethical concerns in a timely manner.

We should uphold the principles of wide participation and consensus-based decision-making, adopt a gradual approach, pay close attention to technological advancements, conduct risk assessments and policy communication, and share best practices. On this basis, we should encourage active involvement from multiple stakeholders to achieve broad consensus in the field of international AI governance, based on exchange and cooperation and with full respect for differences in policies and practices among countries.

We should actively develop and apply technologies for AI governance, encourage the use of AI technologies to prevent AI risks, and enhance our technological capacity for AI governance.

We should increase the representation and voice of developing countries in global AI governance, and ensure equal rights, equal opportunities, and equal rules for all countries in AI development and governance. Efforts should be made to conduct international cooperation with and provide assistance to developing countries, to bridge the gap in AI and its governance capacity. We support discussions within the United Nations framework to establish an international institution to govern AI, and to coordinate efforts to address major issues concerning international AI development, security, and governance.

Glossary

in a bid to	为了,试图
norm *n.*	标准,规范;基准
consensus *n.*	一致看法,共识
premise *n.*	前提,假设
sovereignty *n.*	主权,最高统治权
abide by	遵守;信守;坚持;履行
manipulate *v.*	操纵,摆布;篡改;
disinformation *n.*	故意的假情报;虚假信息

intervene in	干涉,介入
jeopardize *v.*	危及,损害
adhere to	遵守;坚持
malicious *adj.*	恶意的,恶毒的,怀恨的
open-source	开源:提供产品的开源代码的做法;开源软件
supply chain	供应链
monopoly *n.*	垄断,垄断权;垄断企业
unilateral coercive measures	单边强制措施
agile *adj.*	(动作)敏捷的,灵活的;(思维)机敏的
tamper *v.*	做手脚,破坏
algorithm *n.*	(尤指计算机)算法,运算法则
entity *n.*	实体,独立存在体
legitimate *adj.*	正当的,合理的;合法的

 Inference Reading Tasks

Task 1 Answer questions.

(1) What is the likely motivation behind the Global AI Governance Initiative's call for a code of ethics for AI?

(2) What can be inferred about the impact of AI on various industries and sectors?

(3) What measures does the initiative propose to address the challenges of AI?

(4) What can be inferred about the initiative's approach to AI governance?

Task 2 Discuss.

ChatGPT and Sora launched by OpenAI have aroused heated discussion on and great concerns about the possibility of what AI can do. As has stated in the text, the Chinese government calls on all countries to enhance information exchange and technological cooperation on the governance of AI and opposes using AI technologies for the purposes of manipulating public opinion, spreading disinformation, intervening in other countries' internal affairs, social systems and social order, as well as jeopardizing the sovereignty of other states. How will your life be affected by AI, and how should AI governance be applied in your daily life?

Text B

China's Space Program: A 2021 Perspective (Excerpt)

Development of space technology and systems

China's space industry serves its major strategic needs, and targets cutting-edge technology that leads the world. Spearheaded by the major space projects, the country has accelerated research into core technologies, stepped up their application, and redoubled its efforts to develop space technology and systems. As a result, China's capacity to enter and return from space, and its ability to engage in space exploration, utilization and governance have grown markedly along a sustainable path.

1. Space Transport System

From 2016 to December 2021, 207 launch missions were completed, including 183 by the Long March carrier rocket series. The total launch attempts exceeded 400.

The Long March carrier rockets are being upgraded towards non-toxic and pollution-free launch, and they are becoming smarter boosted by modular technology. The Long March-5 and Long March-5B carrier rockets have been employed for regular launches; Long March-8 and Long March-7A have made their maiden flights, with increased payload capacity.

China now provides a variety of launch vehicle services. The Long March-11 carrier rocket has achieved commercial launch from the sea; the Smart Dragon-1, Kuaizhou-1A, Hyperbola-1, CERES-1 and other commercial vehicles have been successfully launched; successful demonstration flight tests on reusable launch vehicles have been carried out.

2. Space Infrastructure

(1) Satellite remote-sensing system

The space-based section of the China High-resolution Earth Observation System has been largely completed, enabling high-spatial-resolution, high-temporal-resolution and high-spectrum-resolution earth observation. China now provides improved land observation services, having launched the Ziyuan-3 03 earth resources satellite, the Huanjing Jianzai-2A/2B satellites for environmental disaster management, a high-resolution multi-mode imaging satellite, a hyper-spectral observation satellite, and a number of commercial remote-sensing satellites.

In ocean observation, China is now able to view multiple indexes of contiguous waters around the globe on all scales, with high-resolution images from the Haiyang-1C/1D satellites and the Haiyang-2B/2C/2D satellites.

China's ability to observe the global atmosphere has achieved a significant increase. Its new-generation Fengyun-4A/4B meteorological satellites in the geostationary orbit are able to perform all-weather, precise and uninterrupted atmospheric monitoring and disaster monitoring to boost response capability. The successful launches of Fengyun-3D/3E satellites enable coordinated morning, afternoon and twilight monitoring, and the Fengyun-2H satellite provides monitoring services for countries and regions participating in the Belt and Road Initiative.

With further improvements to the ground system of its remote-sensing satellites, China is now able to provide remote-sensing satellite data receiving and quick processing services across the world.

(2) Satellite communications and broadcasting system

China has made steady progress in developing fixed communications and broadcasting satellite network, which now covers more areas with greater capacity. The Zhongxing-6C and Zhongxing-9B satellites ensure the uninterrupted, stable operation of broadcasting and television services. The Zhongxing-16 and APSTAR-6D satellites, each with a 50Gbps capacity, signify that satellite communications in China have reached the stage of high-capacity service.

The mobile communications and broadcasting satellite network has expanded with the launch of the Tiantong-1 02/03 satellites, operating in tandem with the Tiantong-1 01 satellite, to provide voice, short message and data services for hand-held terminal users in China, its neighboring areas, and certain parts of the Asia-Pacific.

The relay satellite system is being upgraded with the launch of the Tianlian-1 05 and Tianlian-2 01 satellites, giving a powerful boost to capacity.

The satellite communications and broadcasting ground system has been improved, to form a space-ground integrated network that provides satellite communications and broadcasting, Internet, Internet of Things, and information services around the globe.

(3) Satellite navigation system

The completion and operation of the 30-satellite BeiDou Navigation Satellite System (BDS-3) represents the successful conclusion of the system's three-step strategy and its capacity to serve the world. BeiDou's world-leading services include positioning, navigation, timing, regional and global short-message communication, global search and rescue, ground-based and satellite-based augmentation, and precise point positioning.

3. Manned Spaceflight

The Tianzhou-1 cargo spacecraft has docked with the earth-orbiting Tiangong-2 space laboratory. With breakthroughs in key technologies for cargo transport and in-orbit propellant replenishment, China has successfully completed the second phase of its manned spaceflight project.

The launch of the Tianhe core module marks a solid step in building China's space station. The Tianzhou-2 and Tianzhou-3 cargo spacecraft and the Shenzhou-12 and Shenzhou-13 manned spacecraft, together with the Tianhe core module to which they have docked, form an assembly in steady operation. Six astronauts have worked in China's space station, performing extravehicular activities, in-orbit maintenance, and scientific experiments.

4. Deep Space Exploration

(1) Lunar exploration

Achieving relay communications through the Queqiao satellite, the Chang'e-4 lunar probe performed humanity's first soft landing on the far side of the moon, and conducted roving exploration. The Chang'e-5 lunar probe brought back 1,731 g of samples from the moon, marking China's first successful extraterrestrial sampling and return, and the completion of its three-step lunar exploration program of orbiting, landing and return.

(2) Planetary exploration

The Tianwen-1 Mars probe orbited and landed on Mars; the Zhurong Mars rover explored the planet and left China's first mark there. China has achieved a leap from cislunar to interplanetary exploration.

5. Space Launch Sites and Telemetry, Tracking and Command (TT&C)

(1) Space launch sites

Adaptive improvements have been completed at the Jiuquan, Taiyuan and Xichang launch sites, with new launch pads installed at Jiuquan for the commercial launch of liquid fuel rockets, and the Wenchang Launch Site entering service. China has formed a launch site network covering both coastal and inland areas, high and low altitudes, and various trajectories to satisfy the launch needs of manned spaceships, space station modules, deep space probes and all kinds of satellites. In addition, its first sea launch site has begun operation.

(2) Space TT&C

China's leap from cislunar to interplanetary TT&C communications, with growing space-based TT&C capacity, represents a significant progress. Its space TT&C network has improved to form an integrated space-ground TT&C network providing security, reliability, quick response, flexible access, efficient operation and diverse services. TT&C missions of the Shenzhou and Tianzhou spacecraft series, Tianhe core module, Chang'e lunar probe series, and Tianwen-1 Mars probe have been completed successfully. TT&C station networks for commercial satellites are growing quickly.

6. Experiments on New Technologies

China has launched a number of new technological test satellites, and tested new technologies such as the common platforms of new-generation communications satellites, very high throughput satellites' telecommunication payload, Ka-band communications, satellite-ground high-speed laser communications, and new electric propulsion.

7. Space Environment Governance

With a growing database, China's space debris monitoring system is becoming more capable of collision warning and space event perception and response, effectively ensuring the safety of in-orbit spacecraft.

In compliance with the Space Debris Mitigation Guidelines and the Guidelines for the Long-term Sustainability of Outer Space Activities, China has applied upper stage passivation to all its carrier rockets, and completed end of life active deorbit of the Tiangong-2 and other spacecraft, making a positive contribution to mitigating space debris.

Progress has been made in the search and tracking of near-earth objects and in data analysis. A basic space climate service system is now in place, capable of providing services in space climate monitoring, early warning, and forecasting, and is providing broader applications.

💡 Glossary

cutting-edge *adj.*	领先的
spearhead *v.*	领头，带头
Long March carrier rocket series	长征系列运载火箭
non-toxic *adj.*	无毒的
modular technology	模块化技术
payload capacity	额定载重量；有效负载能力
China High-resolution Earth Observation System	中国高分辨率地球观测系统
high-spatial-resolution, high-temporal-resolution and high-spectrum-resolution earth observation	高空间分辨率、高时间分辨率、高光谱分辨率对地观测
hyper-spectral	高光谱
contiguous *adj.*	连续的；邻近的；接触的
meteorological *adj.*	气象学的
geostationary orbit	地球同步轨道
in tandem	一起，同时
hand-held terminal user	手持终端用户
relay satellite system	中继卫星系统
Internet of Things	物联网
ground-based and satellite-based augmentation	地基和卫星增强
dock *v.*	（宇宙飞船）对接
replenishment *n.*	补充，补给
manned spacecraft	载人航天器
roving exploration	巡视探测

Chang'e-5 lunar probe	嫦娥五号(月球探测器)
extraterrestrial *adj.*	地球外的
cislunar to interplanetary exploration	从地月到行星际探索
Telemetry, Tracking and Command (TT&C)	航天测控
space debris monitoring system	空间碎片监测系统
in-orbit spacecraft	在轨航天器
passivation *n.*	钝化;钝化处理
deorbit *n.*	脱离轨道
near-earth object	近地天体

Inference Reading Tasks

Task 1 Discuss.

In the beginning of the text, it says "China's space industry serves its major strategic needs, and targets cutting-edge technology that leads the world". Please work in groups and discuss the following questions:

(1) What kinds of needs are strategic needs for a country?
(2) What are China's major strategic needs?
(3) How can China's space industry serve these needs?

Task 2: Write.

Please write a composition based on the background information: China, along with other space-faring nations, has contributed to the growing problem of space debris. Your writing should include your opinions on the three questions.

1. Who should be responsible for clearing up space debris? Should it be the nations that generate it, international organizations, or private companies?

2. Should nations be financially penalized for generating excessive space debris? If so, how should this be enforced?

3. What are the potential implications of the increasing amount of space debris? How could this impact future space exploration?

Voice beyond Borders

Text C

Xiaomi[①] (Excerpt)

For all the elegance of the hardware, Xiaomi is at heart a software firm. Its CEO and all of its original co-founders came from software firms, and the company's first product (and only product for the first year of its existence) was an operating system for a mobile phone. MIUI (short for "Mi User Interface" and pronounced, quite by design, "Me-You-I") is a modified version of Android, itself a modified version of Linux. Android, distributed by Google, now runs the majority of the world's smartphones. (Apple's software for the iPhone is the only popular alternative, and Android phones outsell iPhones three to one.) Android is free for vendors to use—Google, its main developer, gives it away to have a presence on smartphones—and within certain restrictions, such as offering Google software, phone manufacturers are free to customize Android.

For most of Android's short life, this option meant little more than altering the style of the interface. If you moved from a Google Nexus to a Samsung Galaxy, not much changed other than the background and the icons—the apps and the experience were very similar. The few firms dedicating serious design resources to their products tended to concentrate on making the hardware better. Software customization was left to the user, by way of the apps we choose to install. What set MIUI apart was that even before Xiaomi had a phone of its own

---

① The author of the text is Clay Shirky, a leading voice on the social and economic impact of Internet technologies. He is Vice Provost for Educational Technologies, NYU; Associate Professor of Journalism and Associate Arts Professor of Interactive Telecommunications, NYU. He is the author of *Cognitive Surplus: Creativity and Generosity in a Connected Age* (2010). His writings appear frequently in *The New York Times*, *The Wall Street Journal*, and *Harvard Business Review*, and his TED Talks have been viewed by millions.

to sell, they set about making the operating system work better than the competition. For the first year of the company's life, their only users were people interested enough to download a copy of MIUI and install it on their existing phones, replacing whatever flavor of Android had come with the phone. These users were pioneering (and geeky), and Xiaomi paid close attention to what they wanted and how they used the phones.

Some of the improvements in MIUI were plain old-fashioned performance tuning. Xiaomi paid particular attention to making MIUI work well on Samsung phones. (Though the firm often gets compared to Apple, their product line and mid-market ambitions are much closer to Samsung's.) By 2011 MIUI was better looking and more responsive when running on Samsung smartphones than Samsung's own version of Android was, and, critically, didn't drain the battery as quickly—a huge, underappreciated part of the user experience generally. Part of the plan with early users was to get testing and feedback, of course, but another part was to get free publicity for the user experience. (Sample tweets from 2011: "I installed MIUI into my [Samsung] N1. It is like fresh air. I am feeling good." "I just installed MIUI, my phone became much more easy to use immediately.") This combination of treating users as both sources of feedback and as amateur marketers continues to this day. Hugo Barra, the Google executive in charge of Android who joined Xiaomi in 2013 to spearhead international expansion, boasts that the company spends almost nothing on traditional advertising, preferring to stage launch events that the press will cover, and helping their users proselytize on behalf of the company.

It is in this last category that Xiaomi excels. Tony Wei, Xiaomi's marketing chief, took me on a tour of the company's offices, and pointed out a cluster of desks where employees were working on advertising. Those employees weren't graphic designers or photographers, they were programmers; in keeping with its founding expertise in software, the company makes its own tools for interacting with its users, and for helping those users interact with the world. The company has thought this through with a thoroughness that almost no other firms take on; even the most plumbing-like activities can offer a platform for user outreach. After installing a new version of MIUI, the confirmation screen offers users the ability to send a message on Sina Weibo (China's Twitter, roughly) that they've just upgraded to a new version.

Of course, none of the marketing would have worked if the product wasn't good, but in the beginning, it didn't have to be perfect. It just had to be better than the other Android phones. As time went on, Xiaomi began adding features that don't appear on ordinary Android phones: a better note-taking app, their own music subscription service, their own cloud-based backup service, a MIUI-specific tool for screening out advertising calls (China does not have a National Do Not Call Registry, unlike the U.S.), and, for Asian sensibilities, a highly customizable set of interface themes, since mobile phones are a far more personal item in China than in the U.S. —both phone cases and the look of the home screen are sites of obsessive self-expression.

There was no one "killer feature", no thing that MIUI users could do that other smartphone users couldn't. Instead, early MIUI users got three things that made a difference. The first two were practical: a better experience without upgrading their hardware, and the attentions of a company that was fanatically solicitous of their feedback, seeking out expert users who agreed to provide weekly critiques of MIUI, even before they had shipped the first version, a pattern that continues to this day.

As the user base has grown from the initial hundred recruits to over a hundred million today, Xiaomi began separating its users into two categories—"fever" fans, who are the most eager for new features and the most technically savvy, and "flood" fans, ordinary users who like Xiaomi's products but can't provide detailed feedback. Fever fans are consulted early, given access to products and services while they are still in the initial testing stages. (Some fever fans have proven themselves so valuable that they have been brought on as consultants.) Flood fans are the ones who get the ordinary Friday updates, and post their comments in the Mi forums. Their opinions are generally less technical, but with hundreds of thousands of them active on the forums and discussing the company on social media, their aggregate opinions are useful to Xiaomi, both as research and as marketing. Xiaomi, in turn, is consistently engaged in online community building, creating national "popcorn" fan events, local Mi Fan communities, and even posting pictures of fake Mi phones they find in electronics markets to warn customers.

MIT economist Eric von Hippel calls this sort of user involvement "lead user innovation". In a number of fields, including cooking, mountain climbing, and industrial robotics, the most intensive users, like the fever fans, often understand the product as well or better than the designers, and the modifications and adaptations made by those users are often good candidates for incorporation into the standard product itself. Bill Joy, a co-founder of Sun Microsystems, once said, "No matter who you are, most of the smart people work for someone else." Lead user innovation is a way to bring some of that outside intelligence to bear. Xiaomi has brought lead user innovation into the mobile phone world; Lei Jun has estimated that something like a third of the features in MIUI come from user requests, and he often credits users with co-designing MIUI.

The third thing Xiaomi created was an ineffable sense of specialness for Xiaomi users, the same sense that companies like Apple, Harley-Davidson, and REI produce in their customers. Doing any two of those things would have given them a product, but not a hugely successful one. The company had to deliver a better experience, be more responsive to its users, and reward them with a sense of their perspicacity in adopting MIUI to set themselves apart in a crowded, cost-conscious market.

Glossary

customize *v.*	订制,改制
interface *n.*	(人机)界面(尤指屏幕布局和菜单)
geeky *adj.*	笨拙的,无趣的;极客化的
tweet *n.*	在推特网上发的帖子,微博
amateur *adj.*	业余爱好者;外行;非专业的
proselytize *v.*	归附,改变信仰
subscription *n.*	(杂志等的)订阅费,(服务的)用户费
screen out	筛选出
National Do Not Call Registry	美国谢绝来电计划
solicitous *adj.*	热切期望的;热心的
ship *v.*	推出(计算机商品);(使)上市
savvy *n.*	实际知识,悟性
aggregate *adj.*	总计的
incorporation *n.*	合并;公司
credit sb. with	认为某人具有某种特质或品质
ineffable *adj.*	不可言喻的;不应说出的;难以形容的
perspicacity *n.*	洞察力;聪颖;睿智

Inference Reading Tasks

Task 1　Answer questions.

(1) How does Xiaomi's business model differ from traditional smartphone manufacturers?

(2) How has Xiaomi's use of social media and online platforms contributed to its growth and popularity?

(3) What is the author's attitude towards Xiaomi? What are the clues you have found in the text to support your answer?

(4) What does Xiaomi's emphasis on user feedback and customization reveal about its corporate culture and values?

Task 2: Discuss.

(1) Combine the information from the text with any relevant knowledge you have about Xiaomi's recent developments. Infer how these developments may impact the company's future strategy and market position.

(2) Compare Xiaomi's marketing and branding strategies with those of other major smartphone brands. Infer how Xiaomi's unique approach has helped it stand out in the market.

Practical Assignment

Please choose a specific aspect of China's tech industry to focus on, such as: Artificial Intelligence (AI) advancements, e-commerce platforms and innovations, digital payments, green technology and sustainability. Then conduct research on your chosen topic, utilizing sources such as academic journals and articles, news and reports from mainstream media, industry reports and white papers, company websites and official announcements, and so on. Gather the relevant data and analyze it to identify trends, challenges, and opportunities in your chosen area of China's tech industry. Based on your research and analysis, please prepare a presentation reporting your findings.

Additional Resources

Digital Resource 7-1

Unit 8

China and Global Governance

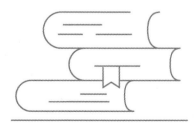

二十大报告选摘

Report to the 20th National Congress of the Communist Party of China (Excerpt)

中国积极参与全球治理体系改革和建设,践行共商共建共享的全球治理观,坚持真正的多边主义,推进国际关系民主化,推动全球治理朝着更加公正合理的方向发展。坚定维护以联合国为核心的国际体系、以国际法为基础的国际秩序、以联合国宪章宗旨和原则为基础的国际关系基本准则,反对一切形式的单边主义,反对搞针对特定国家的阵营化和排他性小圈子。推动世界贸易组织、亚太经合组织等多边机制更好发挥作用,扩大金砖国家、上海合作组织等合作机制影响力,增强新兴市场国家和发展中国家在全球事务中的代表性和发言权。中国坚持积极参与全球安全规则制定,加强国际安全合作,积极参与联合国维和行动,为维护世界和平和地区稳定发挥建设性作用。

China plays an active part in the reform and development of the global governance system. It pursues a vision of global governance featuring shared growth through discussion and collaboration. China upholds true multilateralism, promotes greater democracy in international relations, and works to make global governance fairer and more equitable.

China is firm in safeguarding the international system with the United Nations at its core, the international order underpinned by international law, and the basic norms governing international relations based on the purposes and principles of the *UN Charter*. It opposes all forms of unilateralism and the forming of blocs and exclusive groups targeted against particular countries.

China works to see that multilateral institutions such as the WTO and APEC better play their roles, cooperation mechanisms such as BRICS and the Shanghai Cooperation Organization (SCO) exert greater influence, and emerging markets and developing countries are better represented and have a greater say in global affairs.

China is actively involved in setting global security rules, works to promote international security cooperation, and takes an active part in UN peacekeeping operations. China plays a constructive role in safeguarding world peace and regional stability.

构建人类命运共同体是世界各国人民前途所在。万物并育而不相害,道并行而不相悖。只有各国行天下之大道,和睦相处、合作共赢,繁荣才能持久,安全才有保障。中国提出了全球发展倡议、全球安全倡议,愿同国际社会一道努力落实。中国坚持对话协商,推动建设一个持久和平的世界;坚持共建共享,推动建设一个普遍安全的世界;坚持合作共赢,推动建设一个共同繁荣的世界;坚持交流互鉴,推动建设一个开放包容的世界;坚持绿色低碳,推动建设一个清洁美丽的世界。

Building a human community with a shared future is the way forward for all the world's peoples. An ancient Chinese philosopher observed that "all living things may grow side by side without harming one another, and different roads may run in parallel without interfering with one another". Only when all countries pursue the cause of common good, live in harmony, and engage in cooperation for mutual benefit will there be sustained prosperity and guaranteed security. It is in this spirit that China has put forward the Global Development Initiative and the Global Security Initiative, and it stands ready to work with the international community to put these two initiatives into action.

China is committed to building a world of lasting peace through dialogue and consultation, a world of universal security through collaboration and shared benefits, a world of common prosperity through mutually beneficial cooperation, an open and inclusive world through exchanges and mutual learning, and a clean and beautiful world through green and low-carbon development.

我们真诚呼吁,世界各国弘扬和平、发展、公平、正义、民主、自由的全人类共同价值,促进各国人民相知相亲,尊重世界文明多样性,以文明交流超越文明隔阂、文明互鉴超越文明冲突、文明共存超越文明优越,共同应对各种全球性挑战。

We sincerely call upon all countries to hold dear humanity's shared values of peace, development, fairness, justice, democracy, and freedom; to promote mutual understanding and forge closer bonds with other peoples; and to respect the diversity of civilizations. Let us allow cultural exchanges to transcend estrangement, mutual learning to transcend clashes, and coexistence to transcend feelings of superiority. Let us all join forces to meet all types of global challenges.

Critical Reading Skill—Reflection

Why is reflection important for critical reading?

Reflection is a cognitive process that involves thinking deeply and critically about an experience, a concept, or a piece of information. It is a deliberate and systematic mental activity that allows individuals to gain a deeper understanding of a subject and develop insights. Reflection often involves analyzing, evaluating, and interpreting information, as well as considering personal responses and potential applications. In other words, reflection is a process of thoughtful analysis, evaluation, and interpretation that allows us to engage deeply with information, make meaning of it, and develop our own ideas and understanding.

Reflection is an essential component of critical reading. By honing the reflective skill, we can become more adept at critically analyzing and interpreting a wide range of texts and develop a deeper and more personal understanding of the material. By reflecting, we can better assess the validity and reliability of the information and form our own informed opinions. Reflection also fosters a habit of metacognition, or thinking about our own thinking. This metacognitive awareness allows us to monitor our comprehension, identify areas of confusion or uncertainty, and take steps to address these gaps in understanding.

Tips to train and develop reflection skill:

To develop the important skill of reflection, the following tips are especially helpful.

(1) Reading from another person's viewpoint. Reading passages are often followed by comprehension questions. They focus mainly on understanding the writer's viewpoint, but what is the viewpoint of a different writer or another person? An article about tourism in Ningxia could be quite different by a tour company operator, a hotel developer, a tour guide and a local resident. An article about using animals for research would be very different by an animal rights activist, a hospital doctor, a pharmaceutical company director or by a medical researcher. Thus, try to read the text from the point of view of different roles. Ask yourself

which ideas the person in that role would agree or disagree with and note all the ideas that would support their point of view.

(2) Conversation. Engage in conversations or discussions about the text you read. Share your interpretations, ask questions, and challenge your teacher or classmates' perspectives. Ask probing questions about the text, such as "Why did the author choose to include this detail?" or "What are the implications of this event or campaign?" By starting conversations, asking and answering questions, you can develop a habit of critically reflecting on the text's content and purpose.

(3) Self-evaluation. Evaluate your own viewpoint and describe how it has changed after looking at the topic from different angles. It may help to generate more ideas if you choose to do a written reflection. You might complete sentences such as: Looking at... from a...'s viewpoint helped me to understand... Reading the text from the perspective of a... made me realize that... Re-telling the story from...'s point of view made me think differently about... Then compare your answers in pairs or groups.

Warm-up Questions

1. What is global governance, and is it important?
2. How much do you know about China's involvement in global governance?
3. What role does China play in addressing global challenges such as climate change, poverty, inequality, pandemics and global health crises?

Text

China's Unique Role in the Field of Global Health (Excerpt)

Chinese approaches

China's participation in global health governance

China has always been a strong supporter of and practitioner in the field of global health. Since 1963, China has been sending medical teams to more than 66 developing countries in Africa and other parts of the world. In recent years, China has created the Association of Southeast Asian Nations (ASEAN) Public Health Fund, actively participated in health cooperation efforts between the Asia-Pacific Economic Cooperation (APEC) and the Shanghai Cooperation Organization (SCO), and hosted the first health ministers' meeting of the BRICS countries (Brazil, Russia, India, China, and South Africa) in 2001. China also contributed to the global fund to the extent of USD 30 million by 2002, hosted a fundraiser for Avian Influenza prevention and control in 2006, and donated USD 10 million to UN agencies toward addressing global health issues. After becoming the sixth largest contributor to the UN in 2013, China continued to increase the extent of its voluntary contributions to the WHO and UNAIDS. China is also a member of the decision-making body and expert advisory group at the WHO, UNAIDS, and other major international organizations.

Consistency with local conditions

With abundant experience in fundamental medical and healthcare systems, China can be a role model for other developing countries. China's new rural cooperative medical insurance has expanded significantly. Michel Sidibé, the Executive Director of UNAIDS, said that the UN is learning from the experience of the barefoot doctors of China who are a part of the basic medical insurance initiative in China, and that the UN is planning to train 2 million community health workers in Africa by 2020. With a severe shortage of grassroots doctors and the difficulty in retaining talent, the Tanzanian government has shown high interest in the Barefoot Doctors program. China has extensive experience in training Barefoot Doctors. Many rural doctors are local villagers and serve the local area. This model may be useful for other countries that experience a shortage of talent.

Sharing China's health service experience

China's infant mortality rate (IMR) dropped from 28.38‰ in 2000 to 8‰ in 2017, and the maternal mortality rate dropped from 108.7 per 100,000 persons in 1996 to 21.8 per 100,000 persons in 2015. By 2005, China achieved the global tuberculosis (TB) control target set by WHO, with at least 80% detection rate and successfully treating more than 90% of those patients. China has eliminated lymphatic filariasis, malaria, and schistosomiasis, and implemented a national immunity program; it currently provides free vaccinations to prevent 15 types of diseases that include 4 vaccines for 6 diseases and 5 vaccines for Hepatitis B. All great achievements in public health in China has been supported by solid technologies such as the development of vaccines and drugs, portable ultrasound detection equipment, fetal monitoring equipment, diagnostic reagents, the Shang Ring, Artemisinin, and subepidermal contraceptive implants. Concurrently, China is also a major producer of medicines and medical facilities. With reliable quality and reasonable pricing, medicaments developed and produced in China have drastically supported its public health services. Using only 5% of the world's health resources, China successfully meets the health demands of 20% of the world's population.

Led by the government and guaranteed by policies

In March 2018, during the First Session of the 13th National People's Congress of China, the proposal to reform the State Council and establish the China International Development Cooperation Agency (CIDCA) was passed, which officially opened on April 18, 2018. The agency's primary responsibilities include: (1) developing foreign aid strategies, plans, and policies; (2) coordinating major foreign aid issues; (3) offering suggestions, promoting reforms of foreign aid models, formulating foreign aid programs and plans; and (4) supervising and evaluating the implementation of foreign aid projects.

Building responsible departments

Aiming to create a new type of public health aid team and build its capacity by setting up an expert-steering committee, it is very necessary to build a talent pool and offer specialized training. Meanwhile, developing a guideline on international public health development and cooperation is also helpful. Measures include writing official documents on public health in English, developing and managing international public health development cooperation projects, establishing relevant overseas project departments, and respecting the ethics, etiquette, and culture of international public health development and cooperation. In addition, it seeks to ensure the stability of overseas public health work and the implementation of public health projects, improving communication and negotiation skills used in international public health development cooperation, and understanding international public health strategies.

To improve China-Africa Cooperation in public health, there could be a variety of ways, including regularly communicating and discussing relevant topics, short-term training (10 days) and further study (3 months) programs for the African countries of Belt and Road Initiative, holding seminars, and sending experts to introduce the international public health development aid and enhance capacity to participate.

China's public health aid capacity building projects are solidly supported by the Chinese Center for Disease Control and Prevention (China CDC). First, with the expansion of globalization, world trade, migration, and international exchange activities, global health has become an increasingly important agenda worldwide and for individual countries, as it is closely related to national security, diplomacy, economy and trade, agriculture, and environment. Given the outbreak of emerging and re-emerging communicable diseases in recent years and the public health measures included in many countries' national security strategies, the risk of transnational spread of diseases should also be considered in the course of strategy- and policy-making efforts, training talents, and developing projects.

Second, the world has increasingly high expectations for China, given its peaceful rise and growing power. President Xi has shown a positive attitude and has promoted strong efforts to help African countries and to participate in global health initiatives. These include commitments announced at the 2015 UN General Assembly and the 2015 Summit of the Forum on China-Africa Cooperation to support public health policies and strategies of African countries, and to help them optimize their public health prevention systems. As the infrastructure and capacity of health systems in African countries are weak, especially in West Africa which is still recovering from the Ebola epidemic, the establishment of public health systems and the cultivation of talents become crucial. This provides an opportunity for China to make progress in public health assistance in terms of public health aid, the construction of talent teams, and the establishment of an external supporting environment. It is particularly urgent and necessary to train a team of competent experts and to design a reasonable top structure for cooperative public health projects such as the construction of the African Center for Disease Control and Prevention (Africa CDC) and the establishment of the West African Center for Tropical Disease Research and Control in Sierra Leone.

Third, among the Chinese government's current practices in the field of foreign aid for health, public health aid is still in its early stages. Medical assistance in response to the Ebola outbreak in West Africa in 2014 was the largest foreign public health assistance thus far and revealed numerous problems in policy, management, and fundraising. The process of designing and conducting this project improved drastically and stimulated the completion of China's foreign health aid policies and practices by improving and enriching the policies, mechanisms, teams, practices, and guidelines for public health aid.

Fourth, the China CDC is a leading public health institution in China, and an important technological force in foreign public health assistance. It is responsible for assisting in the Ebola epidemic in West Africa, the construction of the Africa CDC, the technological cooperation with the P3 Laboratory in Sierra Leone, and the control and prevention of malaria. It has accumulated vast expertise in medical aid. The design and implementation of this project is consistent with the Chinese government's commitments to foreign health assistance and China's strategic development goals. However, to meet the needs of public health assistance in the new era, it is necessary to comprehensively and systematically develop and improve the construction of institutions, mechanisms, modes of cooperation, and the capacity of institutions and experts. These initiatives can help solve serious problems and urgent needs that challenge China's exploration of foreign public health assistance in the new era and can help meet the requirements for the construction of public health systems in African countries.

Glossary

Avian Influenza	禽流感
tuberculosis *n.*	结核病
detection rate	检测率
lymphatic filariasis	淋巴丝虫病：一种由丝虫引起的寄生虫病，影响淋巴系统

schistosomiasis *n.*	血吸虫病：一种由血吸虫引起的寄生虫病，影响肝脏和肠道
vaccination *n.*	疫苗接种
Hepatitis B	乙型肝炎
portable ultrasound	便携式超声
fetal monitoring	胎儿监护
diagnostic reagent	诊断试剂
Shang Ring	商环：一种用于男性包皮环切手术的医疗器械
Artemisinin *n.*	青蒿素
subepidermal *adj.*	表皮下的
contraceptive implant	皮下埋植避孕剂
medicament *n.*	药物，药剂
State Council	国务院
China International Development Cooperation Agency	中国国际发展合作署
communicable disease	传染病
General Assembly	联合国大会

 Reflective Reading Tasks

Task 1　Answer the following questions.

（1）Do you think China's healthcare initiatives, such as the rural cooperative medical insurance, are effective, why? And are they applicable to healthcare systems in other developing nations? Can China serve as a role model for other developing countries, and why?

（2）Reflect on China's achievements in public health, including the significant reduction in infant mortality rate, maternal mortality rate, and the successful control of diseases. What are the factors contributing to these achievements?

Task 2 Write an essay.

Analyze the challenges and opportunities in China's foreign health assistance, particularly in the context of its response to the Ebola epidemic in West Africa. Write an essay and reflect on the lessons learned from China's foreign health aid policies and practices and their implications for future global health assistance efforts.

Text B

China's International Development Cooperation in the New Era (Excerpt)

Achieving New Progress in International Development Cooperation

China has continued a steady increase in the scale of its international development cooperation, giving high priority to the least developed countries in Asia and Africa and developing countries participating in the Belt and Road Initiative. To adapt to changes in the domestic and international situation, China has reformed its management system and is exploring new ways to promote international development cooperation with better results.

Steady Growth

China has steadily increased the scale and further expanded the scope of its foreign aid. From 2013 to 2018, China allocated a total of RMB270. 2 billion for foreign assistance in three categories—grants, interest-free loans, and concessional loans. Grants of RMB127. 8 billion, accounting for 47. 3 percent of the total, mainly went to help other developing countries build small and medium-sized social welfare projects and to fund projects for cooperation in human resources development, technical cooperation, material assistance, and emergency humanitarian assistance, as well as projects under the South-South Cooperation Assistance Fund. Interest-free loans of RMB11. 3 billion, constituting 4. 18 percent of the total, were mainly allocated to help developing countries construct public facilities and launch projects for improving local people's lives. Concessional loans of RMB131. 1 billion, making up 48. 52 percent of the total, were provided to help developing countries undertake industrial projects and large and medium-sized infrastructure projects that yield economic and social benefits, and for the supply of technical services, complete sets of equipment, mechanical and electrical products, and other goods and materials. From 2013 to 2018, China extended assistance to 20 regional and international multilateral organizations and 122 countries across the world—30 in Asia, 53 in Africa, 9 in Oceania, 22 in Latin America and the Caribbean, and 8 in Europe.

Diverse Forms

In addition to undertaking complete projects, providing goods and materials, and conducting technical cooperation, China set up the South-South Cooperation Assistance Fund in 2015 to launch development cooperation programs, and continues to explore new models and methods of foreign aid.

—Complete projects. From 2013 to 2018, China undertook the construction of 423 complete projects, with the focus on infrastructure and agriculture. In addition to the traditional "turnkey" model of assistance, China also launched pilot projects in some countries and regions with sound tendering processes and experience in organizing and implementing such projects. Under this model, China provided both funds and technical assistance to those projects, and the recipient countries were responsible for site survey, design, construction, and process management.

China-Funded Complete Projects by Sector and Sector Number of Projects, 2013-2018

Public facilities: 306
hospitals (58) schools (86) civil construction (19)
well-drilling and water supply (20)
public infrastructure (60) others (63)

Economic infrastructure: 80
transport (56) biogas (1)
broadcast and telecommunications (13) electricity (6) others (4)

Agriculture: 19
agricultural pilot centers (5) farmland water conservancy (2)
agricultural processing (6) others (6)

Industry: 5

Climate change programs: 13
wind and solar energy (10) biogas (1) small hydropower (2)

Total: 423

—Goods and materials. From 2013 to 2018, China provided 124 countries and regions with 890 deliveries of goods and materials, most of which comprised mechanical equipment, inspection equipment, transport vehicles, medicine and medical devices.

—Technical cooperation. From 2013 to 2018, China completed 414 such projects in 95 countries and regions, mainly covering industrial production and management, agricultural planting and breeding, culture and education, sports and training, medical and health care, clean energy development, and planning and consulting.

—Cooperation in human resources development. From 2013 to 2018, China held more than 7,000 training sessions and seminars for foreign officials and technical personnel and in-service education programs, training a total of some 200,000 people. Such projects cover more than 100 subjects in 17 fields, including politics and diplomacy, public administration, national development, poverty reduction through agricultural development, medical and health care, education and scientific research, culture and sports, and transport.

Institute of South-South Cooperation and Development

President Xi Jinping announced a plan to establish the Institute of South-South Cooperation and Development (ISSCAD) during the High-Level Roundtable on South-South Cooperation co-hosted by China and the United Nations in September 2015. In April 2016, ISSCAD was set up in Peking University. Its goal is to share China's experience in state governance and train talent from other developing countries to modernize their governance capacity. Since its founding ISSCAD has enrolled around 220 doctoral and master's candidates from 59 developing countries, representing governments, academic institutions, news media and NGOs.

In July 2017, when the first 26 students of ISSCAD graduated with their master's degrees, they read out a thank-you letter to President Xi Jinping. On October 11, Xi wrote back to congratulate them on their graduation, encouraging them to make the best of what they had learned, keep going, aim high, and work hard to explore a sustainable development path suitable for their own countries, and become leaders of reform and development. Xi hoped they would cherish their friendships with teachers, classmates and friends in China, play new roles in promoting friendship and cooperation between China and their countries, and achieve new successes in South-South cooperation.

—South-South Cooperation Assistance Fund. By the end of 2019, China had launched 82 projects under the SSCAF (South-South Cooperation Assistance Fund) framework in cooperation with 14 international organizations, including the United Nations Development

Programme (UNDP), World Food Programme (WFP), World Health Organization (WHO), United Nations Children's Fund (UNICEF), United Nations Population Fund (UNFPA), United Nations High Commissioner for Refugees (UNHCR), International Organization for Migration (IOM), and International Committee of the Red Cross (ICRC). These projects cover agricultural development and food security, poverty reduction, health care for women and children, response to public health emergencies, education and training, post-disaster reconstruction, migrant and refugee protection, and aid for trade.

South-South Cooperation Assistance Fund

In September 2015, President Xi Jinping announced at the United Nations Sustainable Development Summit the creation of the SSCAF with an initial contribution of US $2 billion, to support developing countries in carrying out the UN 2030 *Agenda for Sustainable Development*. In May 2017, President Xi announced an additional contribution of US $1 billion to the SSCAF at the First Belt and Road Forum for International Cooperation in Beijing.

By pooling resources from China and the international community, the SSCAF aims to promote South-South cooperation, and support developing countries in participating in global economic governance on an equal footing. It is an innovative initiative for the Chinese government to champion the 2030 *Agenda* and facilitate sustainable development in other developing countries. It embodies China's effort to value and bolster South-South cooperation, and demonstrates that as a major country, China honors its responsibilities and welcomes other countries to board the express train of its development to achieve common progress.

The SSCAF gives priority to humanitarian aid, agricultural development and food security, health care, poverty alleviation, disaster preparation and mitigation, education and training, sustainable industrial development, eco-environmental protection, trade promotion, and investment facilitation. It focuses on micro and small public wellbeing projects in cooperation with mainly international organizations, think tanks, and social organizations from China and recipient countries.

—Medical teams. By the end of 2019, China had dispatched 27,484 medical workers in 1,069 groups to 72 countries and regions. They worked in all departments of medical and health care, including internal medicine, surgery, gynecology, pediatrics, traditional Chinese medicine, anesthesiology, patient care, pathology, clinical laboratories, and public health. Currently there are nearly 1,000 Chinese medical workers providing assistance at 111 health care facilities in 55 countries across the globe.

—Outbound volunteers. From 2013 to 2018, China dispatched more than 20,000 young volunteers and volunteer Chinese-language teachers to work in over 80 countries around the world.

—Emergency humanitarian aid. From 2013 to 2018, China extended emergency humanitarian assistance to 60 countries. This included providing supplies and equipment, dispatching international rescue teams and medical expert groups, and repairing damaged facilities.

—Debt relief. From 2013 to 2018, China canceled RMB4.18 billion of debts involving 98 mature interest-free loans to least developed countries, heavily indebted poor countries, and landlocked and small island developing countries.

Groundbreaking Progress in Reform and Management

To better adapt to the new circumstances, China has reformed its foreign aid systems and mechanisms to improve management and promote international development cooperation in the new era.

—Institutional reform. In April 2018, the Chinese government set up the China International Development Cooperation Agency (CIDCA) directly under the State Council. This is a significant move to safeguard world peace and promote common development. It serves to better plan and coordinate efforts on international cooperation and build synergy for development. The establishment of such a specialized agency represents a milestone in China's foreign aid journey.

—Better management. China has improved its evaluation mechanisms for foreign aid projects, so as to raise the quality and depth of feasibility analysis. To make feasibility studies more forward-looking, environmental impact, future management and other long-term factors are taken into consideration.

China has formulated clearly defined project management rules and regulations, improved procedures for governmental procurement, contract performance, and qualification assessment of enterprises bidding for foreign aid projects, and endeavored to establish a tendering system focusing on high quality and competitive pricing. To guard against corruption, China has strengthened the performance appraisal mechanism for entities undertaking projects.

China has optimized its rapid response mechanism for emergency humanitarian aid to ensure prompt and effective assistance, and strengthened supervision and evaluation to improve the overall efficiency of its foreign aid.

Glossary

concessional loan	优惠贷款
pilot project	试点项目
tendering	招标
site survey	现场勘查
biogas *n.*	沼气(由残体植物产生的甲烷等可燃气体)
hydropower *n.*	水力发电
mitigation *n.*	缓解,减轻
gynecology *n.*	妇科
pediatrics *n.*	儿科
debt relief	债务减免
interest-free loan	无息贷款
landlocked *adj.*	无海岸线或海港的;内陆的
governmental procurement	政府采购
contract performance	合同履行
bidding for	投标
appraisal *n.*	评估,估价

Reflective Reading Tasks

Task 1 Ask questions.

(1) China has significantly increased its foreign aid. What questions do you want to ask concerning its assistance in grants, interest-free loans, and concessional loans for development and infrastructure projects in recipient countries?

(2) China's foreign aid includes complete projects, goods and materials provision, technical cooperation, and human resources development. What questions should China ask

when such aid is going to be provided?

(3) Reflect on the establishment and impact of the South-South Cooperation Assistance Fund (SSCAF) in supporting developing countries in carrying out the *UN 2030 Agenda* for Sustainable Development. What questions would you like to raise regarding the priority areas of assistance and the collaborative efforts with international organizations to achieve common progress?

Task 2　Make a speech.

Conduct in-depth research on China's international development cooperation initiatives, including its foreign aid programs, infrastructure projects, and partnerships with developing countries, and deliver a persuasive and well-reasoned speech titled "China's International Development Cooperation: Challenges, Opportunities, and Global Impact".

Voice beyond Borders

Text C

Understanding China's Growing Involvement in Global Health and Managing Processes of Change (Excerpt)

Conclusions: experimentation and innovation for global health

In the late 1970s, as China started to launch market reforms, it did so in a pragmatic way, which allowed experimentation and learning about what might work in its distinct institutional, political and economic environment. In doing so, the country adopted a number of unorthodox approaches and started a process of gradual and experimental transition to a new (though not finally or fully defined) state. Experimentation has played an important role in subsequent reforms to the economy, state, political and administrative structure, and society. This has enabled China to achieve rates of development that would have been considered by almost all experts to be impossible. A similar process at the global level is now starting as the leadership encourages a rapid increase in China's role in international development, including health. As with so many rounds of previous reforms, high-level aims (targets and aspirations) are set out in national strategies and leadership speeches. These encourage implementing agencies to carry out widespread experimentation and innovation to create the means needed to achieve them.

Unpacking the concept of means shows the necessity of experimentation, innovation and learning on multiple fronts. As outlined above, this is already taking place in areas including exploration of China's historical approaches to health assistance, reflection on the usefulness of these approaches in the early twenty-first century, and their significance given the new context of China's rapidly increasing engagement and debates regarding what China's new global role should be.

These experiences have shown the need for widespread development of capacity to perform the kinds of tasks (for example in research, analysis, support to decision- and policy-making) required by China's increasing global health engagement. They have also shown the need for new kinds of linkage between agencies, including various functional networks (e.g. networks linking universities developing courses and research on global health), links between government and non-government agencies (e.g. between the NHC and research agencies), between different parts of government (e.g. the NHC and new agencies such as CIDCA) and between Chinese agencies and international partners (e.g. WHO, DFID).

Many Chinese health agencies are increasing their capacity to provide the new kinds of analysis needed by decision makers. Initiatives such as the 2015-2017 BRI health cooperation plan show how highly pluralistic, emergent initiatives across the country are being screened and assessed for their usefulness as potential models for a more diversified Chinese role in global health. CIDCA and the SSCAF are institutional innovations intended to support new initiatives by Chinese and external agencies (notably UN agencies) and explore new cooperation modalities outside the constraints of the current Chinese institutional system. However, this is only a beginning. These agencies still employ a small number of people with the expertise and experience they need. This is likely to change over the next few years.

The breadth of recent leadership commitments makes clear the need for continued exploration, innovation and learning if Chinese agencies are to fulfil the ambitions of the leadership for greater engagement. As we have argued, China has historically employed approaches to rapid experimentation and learning in managing domestic reforms. Approximately five years on from the beginning of implementation of the GHSP, there is now considerable ferment in China's global health engagement and a proliferation of new initiatives.

How China engages globally is of significance to the world, not just China. Chinese engagement—for example in Africa—most recently badged as Belt and Road Initiative, has stimulated a great deal of analysis. There is criticism, as well as analyses that point to the positive potential of China's changing global engagement. Countries typically have a variety of motivations for engaging in development cooperation and global health including geopolitical, commercial interests and domestic political concerns as well as a recognition of the importance of certain global public goods. The actions of China will increasingly have an impact on global health and that country will, in turn, be increasingly exposed to risks associated with its dense networks of global communication. These are important issues that merit additional research and analysis. This paper does not attempt to assign weights to the different motivations of global health actors. Its focus is on areas of widespread agreement on global health objectives and on the serious negative consequences of a failure to cooperate. It argues that a significant effort will be needed to build effective collaboration and avoid these deleterious outcomes.

China's engagement in global health comes at a time of very rapid change as rapid global development leads to new public health challenges, while a number of developed countries either retrench or refashion their assistance portfolios. There is little doubt that there is a need for increased resources and new solutions to global health problems. The Chinese leadership is intent on greater cooperation in this area, and programmes such as the GHSP show the significance attached by other countries, UN agencies and the like to work with China as an emerging actor in development. The medium- to long-term outcomes of such collaborations and China's increasing engagement in development and health will be strongly influenced by the willingness and capacity of Chinese institutions to learn from these new experiences and adapt their policies and practices, as well as by the willingness and capacity of "incumbent" agencies to adapt.

Recent years have seen an increase in attention to the rise of new development actors and the distinct developmental experience or approaches they bring, as well as the increasing significance of south-south learning and policy transfer. Much of the focus has been on policy transfer and learning at the level of particular practices or policy models. This paper has discussed a higher-level phenomenon—approaches that are not specific to one particular technical area, but concern system-level institutions or rules that guide the ways that change is managed.

The *2015 World Development Report* pointed out many heuristics and biases of the global development community, arguing that these color the ways that development professionals see the world, its problems, and potential solutions. With the increasing engagement of countries such as China in global development, the "development community" will surely become more diverse, bringing a wider range of world views to bear when trying to solve problems. As development and global health debates diversify, there is increasingly a need for new forms of understanding—for Chinese development and global health professionals to understand the global system and how to engage in it, and for professionals from established donor countries, multilateral agencies and low and middle-income countries to better understand the approaches, thinking and development experiences that their new peers bring.

Practically speaking, there is a need for experimentation and learning in the context of the rapid social, economic and environmental change that is currently underway. The major investments funded as part of the Belt and Road Initiative are likely to strengthen and deepen regional and global connectivity, resulting in new public health challenges—and new possibilities for addressing them. The GHSP provided modest levels of support for an initial stage of learning that has principally helped inform change in China. As China's global footprint increases, there is a need for initiatives that create the learning needed by multiple partners and agencies regarding how to work together to deal with global challenges. Several programmes, including the GHSP, have started to provide evidence on how experimental initiatives can foster this kind of learning. There is now a need for initiatives and substantial investment in new approaches to learning about the management of change. Potential bilateral and multi-lateral partners will need to make a substantial effort to build their capacity to collaborate effectively with China, as China will need to build capacity to collaborate with others. It may take a lot of time and effort to agree on global decision-making processes and, meanwhile, effective responses to disease challenges could be delayed. However, the alternative would be a long-term fragmentation of public health efforts.

The emergence of a new global power inevitably disrupts established ways of doing global governance. This is taking place in a period of rapid change that is presenting major challenges that require global cooperation. The challenge for China, other global actors and multilateral organization is to find ways to incorporate new approaches to global collaboration, while maintaining the stability of existing governance arrangements for global health. This will require willingness on all sides to learn from each other and invest the effort needed to build governance arrangements appropriate for the coming decades. This is not only important as a means of protecting global public health, but also as a demonstration of how governance arrangements can be adapted to the needs of a pluralistic global order in a context of rapid change. This is the challenge the new emerging global community faces as it attempts to build a cooperative approach for controlling the COVID-19 pandemic.

 **Glossary**

unorthodox *adj.*	非正统的,非传统的
NHC	国家卫生健康委员会 National Health Commission
CIDCA	国家国际发展合作署 China International Development Cooperation Agency

DFID		英国国际发展署 Department for International Development
pluralistic *adj.*		多元化的,多元论的
emergent *adj.*		新兴的,处于发展初期的
modality *n.*		形式,模式
ferment *n.*		发酵,巨浪,沸腾
proliferation *n.*		大量增加,快速增长
retrench *v.*		减少,紧缩
refashion *v.*		调整,重新设计
portfolio *n.*		投资组合
incumbent *adj.*		现有的
heuristics *n.*		启发,探索

Reflective Reading Tasks

Task 1 Answer questions.

(1) Before reading Text C, what did you know about China's involvement in global health governance? After reading the text, what do you realize?

(2) What is GHSP? And why is it included by the author to support his idea?

(3) If you are going to talk with someone on China's involvement in global health governance, who will you choose, a government official involved in health policy and international relations, an expert in global health governance and international development, a doctor or representative from Chinese health agencies engaged in global health initiatives, a scholar specialized in China's global health engagement, an official from international organizations collaborating with China on global health issues, such as the World Health Organization (WHO), or a patient in another country that was cured by the Chinese medical aid team? And what do you think are the perspective differences of the above-mentioned people on this issue?

Task 2　Debate.

Debate topic: The Role of Experimentation and Learning in China's Global Health Engagement

Debate Proposition: Experimentation and learning are essential for China's effective and sustainable engagement in global health, and are crucial for fostering effective collaboration and governance in the context of rapid global change. Two teams, each representing a different perspective on the proposition, will present their opening statements. The affirmative team will argue in favor of the proposition, emphasizing the importance of experimentation and learning in China's global health engagement. The negative team will present their opposing viewpoint, challenging the significance of experimentation and learning in this context. Both teams will present evidence, case studies, and analysis to support their respective positions, drawing on examples of China's global health initiatives and the impact of experimentation and learning on global health governance.

Practical Assignment

Public Opinion Survey

You can follow the steps below:

◇ Design a structured survey questionnaire that includes questions related to public awareness of China's climate action plan, perceptions of the ambitious targets, and attitudes towards the strategies and achievements highlighted in the plan.

◇ Identify the target audience for the survey, which may include students, community members, or individuals from diverse demographic backgrounds to ensure a representative sample.

◇ Implement the survey by conducting interviews or distributing the questionnaire to the identified target audience. You may use online survey platforms, conduct in-person interviews, or utilize other appropriate methods to gather responses.

◇ Analyze the data to identify trends, patterns, and variations in public awareness, perceptions, and attitudes towards China's climate action plan. You are supposed to use statistical tools and qualitative analysis to interpret the survey results.

◇ Based on the survey findings, prepare a report that summarizes the key insights, trends, and variations in public opinion regarding China's climate action plan.

◇ Share the survey results with your peers. Discuss the implications of public opinion on climate action, and explore potential strategies for enhancing public awareness and engagement with climate initiatives.

Digital Resource 8-1

与本书配套的二维码资源使用说明

本书部分课程及与纸质教材配套数字资源以二维码链接的形式呈现。利用手机微信扫码成功后提示微信登录,授权后进入注册页面,填写注册信息。按照提示输入手机号码,点击获取手机验证码,稍等片刻收到4位数的验证码短信,在提示位置输入验证码成功,再设置密码,选择相应专业,点击"立即注册",注册成功。(若手机已经注册,则在"注册"页面底部选择"已有账号? 立即登录",进入"账号绑定"页面,直接输入手机号和密码登录。)接着提示输入学习码,需刮开教材封面防伪涂层,输入13位学习码(正版图书拥有的一次性使用学习码),输入正确后提示绑定成功,即可查看二维码数字资源。手机第一次登录查看资源成功以后,再次使用二维码资源时,只需在微信端扫码即可登录进入查看。(如申请二维码资源遇到问题,可联系宋焱:15827068411。)